FOR BILL —

I AM VERY FORTUNATE TO
HAVE KNOWN YOU FOR ALL
THESE YEARS —

YOU ARE THE MAN OTHERS
SEEK TO FIND WHEN THEY
LOOK FOR A FRIEND —

THANK YOU FOR STAYING
IN TOUCH WITH ME —

YOUR FRIEND,

David

What People Are Saying about *My Tour in Hell*

"Powell describes his tour in Vietnam with the Marines in great detail which sets the stage for his personal journey home with all the painful memories and problems that surface with someone who has gone to hell and come back to tell about it.

"His autobiographical work is a must read for veterans who remain stuck between two worlds—the physical reality of civilian life while the psychological, emotional and spiritual life remain on the battlefield half a world away. Healing is painful but so necessary to reintegrate those two worlds into one. Healing is not forgetting; healing is making sense of the past in order to live life in the present with a restored hope for the future. Powell articulates this process very well and has given a tremendous gift to the combat veteran community of any generation."

>Father Philip G. Salois, M.S.
>Founder, International Conference of War Veteran Ministers
>(*formerly the National Conference of Viet Nam Veteran Ministers*)
>National Chaplain, Vietnam Veterans of America

"The connection of David's problems in his current life and his Viet Nam experiences is one of the clearest descriptions of how trauma affects our lives I have ever read. *My Tour in Hell* is a tribute to David's unwillingness to give up on himself in the face of great unhappiness."

>—Laura W. Groshong, LICSW (Seattle, WA)

"Years in combat zones, group psychotherapy with combat vets diagnosed with PTSD and TIR training qualifies me to recommend this book. *My Tour in Hell* attests to David's journey from the boundary of a Marine grunt's PTSD despair to the horizon of integration, risk, and new meaning. Those in the helping professions will learn how the negative emotional 'charge' of trauma can be partially or totally eliminated through the adept facilitation of Traumatic Incident Reduction."

>—Sister Kateri Koverman, LISW, ICDC

"Powell presents a brutally honest and riveting account of one man's descent into the dehumanizing realities of war. However, the journey is worth it to relive his dramatic ascension and redemption from the abyss through the life changing, powerful, and therapeutic techniques of Traumatic Incident Reduction."

>— Rev. James W. Clifton, LCSW, PhD

"Powell begins and ends with hope, and with a method that helped him to finally, and fully, resolve the many traumas he endured. He gives the reader a litany of incidents of trauma, and shows how the whole context of the battlefields, surrounding regions, and finally even home comes under the cloud of a hell many men and women shared with him, a hell that is being created many thousands of times in modern times. The book deserves to be read by therapists, veterans, and their loved ones."
—Rene Ely, M.Div., LMFT

"*My Tour in Hell* is an insightful insider's view of the traumatic events that occurred during the Vietnam War and the devastating after-effects that can follow. For those not familiar with the symptoms of PTSD, this was a vivid and clear view of how this disorder disrupts the lives of those who suffer from it untreated. Definitely a valuable read for anyone who works with this population or who have family or friends who are struggling with PTSD."   —Kirsten Krohn, MFT

"Not every ex-soldier suffers from post-traumatic stress disorder. The ones who do are the sensitive, caring people exposed to the brutalizing conditions of war. David Powell is one of these people, as becomes obvious to the reader of his book.

With young men and women currently exposed to danger in the Middle East, this veteran's story is relevant to today. With utter honesty and integrity, he shows the terrible effects of war. However, his story ends on a high note, because Traumatic Incident Reduction has finally allowed him to cope with the consequences."
—Robert Rich, MSc, PhD, M.A.P.S., A.A.S.H.

"David Powell's book held my interest throughout the entire read. As a therapist working with US military, I was particularly intrigued by the therapeutic technique utilized and would love to have the opportunity for training. I was most impressed that the author did not present himself as totally recovered, but as functionally recovered with a new quality of life. I will definitely use the book with soldiers and family members."
—Sally Wright, LMFT (Baumholder, Germany)

"This book provides a first-person account of how combat trauma evolves and is a testament to the power of Traumatic Incident Reduction. *My Tour in Hell* is an invaluable resource for working with combat trauma survivors."   —Judy Bronson, PhD, NCC

"David's story demonstrating how possible it is for anyone who has suffered traumatic stress to have healing and recovery vis-à-vis Traumatic Incident Reduction. We plan to start an 'Adopt a Veteran' program so any Vet who wants a copy of your book can have same."

—Mary Murphy, MA, NHA, Former VA and Prison Chaplain

"*My Tour In Hell* is a riveting account of unimaginable pain, suffering, and healing. David Powell takes the reader step by step through his painful metamorphosis from a young, idealistic recruit to an uncaring, angry trauma survivor, and finally to an inspiring, compassionate crusader. His message is one of hope and healing. Through the use of Traumatic Incident Reduction (TIR), David is able to process and release the toxic memories of his tour in Vietnam. His story will challenge the belief that people cannot heal from horrific circumstances. TIR provides a gentle methodology for confronting traumatic images and then releasing them, enabling the user to move the memories into the past. One only wishes that he had encountered this treatment modality much earlier in life, before suffering through the many years of broken relationships, lost jobs, and substance abuse."

—Patricia Sherman, Ph.D., LCSW   www.HealingIsPossible.com

"I picked up this book one night and couldn't let go of it until 3:00AM. I served in the Israeli Defense Force and it brought back so many memories! This book offers one of the best, most intimate descriptions of Post Traumatic Stress Disorder (PTSD) that I have ever read precisely because the author is a fellow sufferer, not a smug psychiatrist or theoretician. His style of prose—direct, matter-of-fact, and unflinchingly honest—also helps. Above all, this book is about hope. There are glimpses of humanity amidst the worst atrocities and there are effective therapies to coax the victims of war back into peace and life. It worked for the author who has endured decades of trauma-induced ruination and instability in everything from marriage to business. If he was salvaged, so can us all."

—Sam Vaknin, PhD, author of *Malignant Self Love: Narcissism Revisited*

'*My Tour in Hell* is a wrenching book to read as the author bares his soul, revealing the gruesome details of his combat experiences and the personal aftermath as he struggled for decades to deal with the PTSD blighting his life. His final recovery through innovative therapy is a triumph and a new beginning. Read it to better understand the Vietnam Vet and the little support they got after their tour in Hell."

—Chuck Chriss, www.Olive-Drab.com

"*My Tour in Hell* is the first book in *The Reflections of History Series*. It is a very powerfully written autobiography by David W. Powell about his horrific experiences while serving in Vietnam and how his life drastically changed upon his return to the states. The horrors that Powell had to endure while in Vietnam caused him to experience Post Traumatic Stress Disorder (PTSD). As a result of this disorder, he is unable to maintain steady employment, healthy relationships, and he has difficulties with his emotions. The disorder also affects his ability to sleep, and keeps him stuck in a hypervigilant state.

"I highly recommend this book for people who are either experiencing PTSD or are close to someone that has it. I think that Rehabilitation Counselors who work with military veterans would also benefit from reading this because it will give them a greater understanding of what these veterans have gone through. War Veterans would also gain something from reading this book because they will find that they are not alone in dealing with the trauma created by their experiences.

"I asked a disabled Marine Vet if I should share this book with my nephew while he is in Iraq. I wasn't sure if it would be too much for him to read while he is involved in combat. The Marine felt that it would be good for him because it talks about the problems and symptoms that he might experience and most importantly how to deal with them. *My Tour in Hell* shows that there is hope for people that are experiencing PTSD."

—Paige Lovitt for *Reader Views* (5/06)

"This book could be helpful for some Vietnam vets that I saw in an earlier work setting. The book is well-suited to the audience of is folks struggling with combat-related PTSD. Powell is succinct, sometimes blunt in his writing. This is not great flowery prose, but it is not intended to be either. We certainly have a political environment that is averse to making comparisons between Iraq and Vietnam. Powell remains free of the politics involved which will allow his words to reach a wider audience."

—Jason Hobbs, LCSW, MDiv

My Tour in Hell

A Marine's Battle with Combat Trauma

By David W. Powell

Book #1 in the *Reflections of History Series*

Modern History Press

An Imprint of Loving Healing Press

My Tour in Hell: A Marine's Battle with Combat Trauma

Book number one of the Reflections in History Series

First Edition: July 4th, 2006

Library of Congress Cataloging-in-Publication Data

Powell, David Warren, 1941-
  My tour in hell : a Marine's battle with combat trauma / by
David W. Powell.
       p. cm. --   (Reflections of history series ; v. 1)
  Includes bibliographical references and index.
  ISBN-13: 978-1-932690-22-4 (case laminate : alk. paper)
  ISBN-10: 1-932690-22-0 (case laminate : alk. paper)
  ISBN-13: 978-1-932690-23-1 (trade pbk. : alk. paper)
  ISBN-10: 1-932690-23-9 (trade pbk. : alk. paper)
 1. Powell, David Warren, 1941---Mental health. 2. United
States. Marine Corps--Biography. 3. Post-traumatic stress
disorder--Patients--Biography. 4. Vietnamese Conflict, 1961-
1975--Personal narratives, American. 5. Disabled veterans--
United States--Biography. 6. Vietnamese Conflict, 1961-1975-
-Psychological aspects. I. Title. II. Series.
  RC552.P67P69 2006
  362.196'852120092--dc22

2006003924

Distributed by: Baker & Taylor, Ingram Book Group
Modern History Press is an imprint of
Loving Healing Press
5145 Pontiac Trail
Ann Arbor, MI 48105
USA

http://www.LovingHealing.com or
info@LovingHealing.com
Fax +1 734 663 6861

Modern History Press

Reflections of History Series

From
Modern History Press

This series provides a venue for contemporary authors who have lived through significant times in history to reflect on the impact of events and lessons they learned from them.

1. *My Tour in Hell: A Marine's Battle with Combat Trauma* by David W. Powell

2. *Made in America, Sold in the 'Nam: Stories, Poems, and Essays* (2nd Edition), Ed. by Paul Richards

"Those who cannot remember the past
are condemned to repeat it."
George Santayana in *Life of Reason* (1905)

About our Series Editor, Robert Rich, Ph.D.

Loving Healing Press is pleased to announce Robert Rich, Ph.D. as Series Editor for the Reflections of History Series. This exciting new series brings you real-life stories from those who have witnessed and participated in significant events in living history.

Robert Rich, M.Sc., Ph.D., M.A.P.S., A.A.S.H. is a highly experienced counseling psychologist. His web site www.anxietyanddepression-help.com is a storehouse of helpful information for people suffering from almost any way we can make ourselves and each other unhappy.

Bob is also a multiple award-winning writer of both fiction and non-fiction, and a professional editor. His writing can be found at www.bobswriting.com. You are advised not to visit him there unless you have the time to get lost for a while.

Two of his books are tools for psychological self-help: *Anger and Anxiety: Be in Charge of your Emotions and Control Phobias* and *Personally Speaking: Single Session Email Therapy*. However, his philosophy and psychological knowledge come through in all his writing, which is perhaps why three of his books have won international awards, and he has won many minor prizes. Dr. Rich currently resides in Wombat Hollow in Australia.

Table of Contents

Photos, Maps, and Illustrations

Acknowledgments

There are a few people I would like to acknowledge for the direct and indirect support they gave me to help me write my memoir.

Victor R. Volkman, a fine gentleman and highly experienced editor, publisher, and writing coach, contributed greatly to my writing efforts. Victor helped me elaborate and expound upon many portions of this book. Without his skills, patience, and gentle guidance while I struggled with the first draft, and multiple revisions to sections and whole themes of this book, I would have stopped and never finished a first draft of this memoir. He is extremely good at coaxing the hidden truths in an episode onto the written page which I would have otherwise ignored and omitted. He helped me see the reason for writing in that way. Thank you, Sir!

Marian Volkman, a Facilitator par excellence, and wife of Mr. Volkman, contributed her unseen background support of her husband, who subliminally communicated encouragement and praise to me via Victor, throughout the development of this work.

Dr. Bob Rich, a gifted writing coach and excellent editor, who contributed greatly to the approach, restructuring, and emphasis of my writing. He knew how to tell me what I was *not telling you, the reader,* what I should be telling you, and explained it to me in such a way that I was able to complete this endeavor.

Gerald French, a fine gentleman and friend, who contributed to my mental health recovery as he played the role of my "Facilitator" and I the "Viewer" over the course of time we spent in one-on-one Traumatic Incident Reduction (TIR) therapy sessions in Menlo Park, California in 1989. Without his skills and professional abilities, I would not have been able to retrieve more than a few obscured, unresolved traumatic episodes I experienced in Vietnam.

Tom Joyce, a good friend, excellent listener, and fine author, befriended me during my time spent with Mr. French, and afterwards, as I was engaged in the TIR process. I am extremely grateful that he wrote the Foreword to this memoir. I am also proud that he let me quote a passage he crafted, which discusses my recovery of a buried traumatic experience.

Pieter Van Aggelen, a friend and fellow combat-experienced Marine Infantryman, who introduced me to Mr. French.

Terry Tully, a friend and fellow combat-experienced Marine Infantry-man, who served in the same Da Nang war zone in 1968 that I did in 1967. He encouraged me to submit my PTSD claim to the Veterans Administration and Social Security.

Joe Miller, a combat-experienced American whom I met in the VA group in Menlo Park, California, and remains a friend to this day.

Last, and first of all Susan M. Dettlaff, a beautiful woman, whose heart is bigger than "all outdoors." She quietly stood by my side as I worked on this piece. She endured, without mentioning it to me, the darkness, sadness, and pain I experienced as I retrieved these memories, re-experienced them, and filed them back in my memory bank.

To the other relatives, friends, and associates whose names I did not mention in this acknowledgement, I offer my profound apologies and regret that I inadvertently made no mention of you.

Foreword by Tom Joyce

I remember thinking he was the kind of guy you'd expect to see key-noting a sales convention. Executive material—smartly dressed; blue-eyed; mid-forties; strong, square jaw and neatly trimmed blond hair. To look at him, you'd never have suspected that David Powell had literally been through hell.

It was April of 1989, and I was attending a conference of the Institute for Research in Metapsychology in San Francisco, where my friends, Gerald French and Dr. Frank A. Gerbode, were reporting on a technique they called Traumatic Incident Reduction, or TIR. On Saturday afternoon, David Powell—a Lance Corporal with Delta Company, 1st Battalion, 7th Marines of the 1st Marine Division at Chu Lai and Da Nang—spoke most eloquently about his combat experiences in Vietnam between October 1966 and November 1967, his subsequent years of struggling with the nightmare of post-traumatic stress disorder [PTSD], and his rough-shod treatment at "Club Fed"—the Veterans' Administration state-of-the art hospital in Menlo Park during the late 1980s. "It was not as advertised," David reported, contrasting the VA's medieval approach with his hi-tech experience as a TIR "viewer". I was hooked.

TIR has its roots in Josef Breuer's "talking cure—a recalling or re-experiencing of stressful or disturbing situations or events which appear to have precipitated a neurosis."[1] Sigmund Freud used it as his working model for psychoanalysis, noting that the key to a recent disturbance lay in an *earlier,* similar trauma, sometimes an entire chain of incidents.[2] But Gerbode and French went a step further, employing repetitive and gradient aspects of Behavior Therapy "desensitization," and wrapping it compassionately in Carl Rogers' "person-centered" model, wherein a therapist refrains from offering any authoritative interpretation of his client's experiences. In TIR, the patient/doctor model is obviated: a client is the "viewer" and his therapist is the process "facilitator".

It seemed to have worked wonders for David. After his presentation, I collared him in the hotel lobby and asked if he'd be willing to let me inter-view him in depth about his experiences. David agreed, and we spent hours together. He began to introduce me to other vets he'd met at the Menlo Park facility, and six months later, I'd taped interviews with twenty-odd soldiers, psychiatrists, and VA staff—including the director of their

PTSD program. This visceral, eye-opening exploration culminated in a piece called "Back Into the Heart of Darkness", which was subsequently rejected by *Rolling Stone*, *Mother Jones*, *Playboy*, *Penthouse*, *Atlantic Monthly*, and *Harper's* as "biased."

But in retrospect, bias turned out to be a euphemism for compassion fatigue. In August of 1990, our young men and women began leaving for Saudi Arabia to form a "Desert Shield" along the border of Kuwait against the evil Republican Guard of Saddam Hussein, and nobody in the American media wanted to hear the complaints of traumatized Vietnam "losers" at a time like that.

•   •   •

Richard M. Nixon wrote, "No event in American History is more misunderstood than the Vietnam War. It was misreported then, and it is misremembered now. Rarely have so many people been so wrong about so much. Never have the consequences of their misunderstanding been so tragic."[3]

Despite my differences of opinion with our late, former president on most other issues, I couldn't agree more with his statement about Vietnam. But then, I was sitting in a high school classroom at the time, while David Powell was *there*—literally in the thick of it. Insult was added to injury when he came home to public condemnation instead of a tickertape parade, and then spent the next thirty years having to contend with popular myths and misconception about the undeclared war he'd fought in the jungles of Southeast Asia.

It needs to be said that the American military did *not* lose the war against the North Vietnamese Army [N.V.A.] and Viet Cong. In fact, the accord calling for a peaceful reunification of the country was signed in Paris on 27 January 1973. All parties agreed to a stalemate. The last American troops departed on 29 March 1973, and the Army of the Republic of Vietnam [A.R.V.N.] held Saigon until 30 April 1975, when it fell—quite violently—to the N.V.A., who had signed the treaty.[4]

Contrary to popular misconception, two-thirds of the men and women who served in Vietnam were volunteers, whereas two-thirds of those in World War II were drafted.[5] And despite my own educational deferment, the Vietnam War was not fought by the poor and uneducated: 79

percent of the troops had a high school education or better. It's also a myth that a disproportionate number of African-Americans were killed in combat: 12.5 percent of the casualties were black, 86 percent were white, and 1.2 percent were of other races.[6]

It's been implied—often by vets of other conflicts—that the fighting in Vietnam was less intense than World War II. But in fact, the average infantryman in Vietnam had to face 240 days of combat in a one-year period, while the average South Pacific G.I. saw 40 days in four years.[7] Of the 2.59 million Americans who served in Vietnam between 1964 and 1973—about a million of whom saw combat—58,169 were killed, and 304,000 were wounded. The percentage of amputations and crippling wounds was 300 percent higher than in World War II. 75,000 Vietnam veterans were physically disabled,[8] and according to a four-year study conducted by the Research Triangle Institute for the Veterans' Administration, an estimated 480,000 suffer from post-traumatic stress disorder.

PTSD is not unique to Vietnam Veterans. During World War II, not only was the pre-induction psychiatric rejection rate nearly four times higher than that of World War I, psychiatric casualties were 300 percent higher[9] but were accorded non-clinical terms like "shell shock" and "battle fatigue". At one point in the early 1940s, more men were being discharged for "war neurosis" than were being drafted.[10] 23 percent of the men who suffered from battlefield psychological breakdowns never returned to combat. During the Korean War, owing to immediate on-site treatment provided, psychiatric evacuations dropped to six percent of total casualties. But in Vietnam, psychological breakdowns were at an *all-time low*—only twelve per thousand.[11]

An acronym called DEROS [Date of Expected Return from Over Seas]—meaning a soldier's tour of duty only lasted twelve months, or thirteen if he was a Marine— contributed to this apparent improvement. So did drugs like marijuana, opium, and heroin. And soldiers caught self-medicating were given swift administrative discharges. Thus the whole question of psychological trauma was neatly—and deceptively—avoided. The Defense Department's official neuropsychiatric casualty rate in Vietnam was significantly lower than in either Korea or World War II.[12]

But DEROS had its downside: in contrast to World War II, where men spent weeks—sometimes months—returning from battle, decompressing aboard ships, sharing their experiences with understanding peers, and were honored as heroes when they arrived back home, the Vietnam veteran endured a solitary flight and hometown hostilities. While the elation of survival suppressed early symptoms of PTSD in most Vietnam veterans, for far too many, feelings of restlessness, mistrust, and cynicism evolved into depression, insomnia, flaring tempers, and a morbid obsession with memories of combat.

It wasn't until the mid-1970s that the Forgotten Warrior Project, funded by the Disabled American Veterans, produced a landmark study of the long-term social consequences of combat exposure. As a result, PTSD was formally recognized by the American Psychiatric Association in 1980.

Although its etiology is still passionately debated, the symptoms of PTSD are broadly acknowledged to include flashbacks, nightmares, hyperarousal, exaggerated startle reaction, explosive outbursts, extreme vigilance, irritability, panic symptoms, and sleep disturbance. Complications often include alcohol and drug abuse, chronic anxiety, unemployment, divorce, depression, and increased risk for suicide. In 1988, it was estimated that 40 percent of Vietnam veterans had a drug problem, and nearly half had been divorced at least once.[13]

•   •   •

As a result of my enthusiastic "bias" toward the efficacy of TIR in treating the root cause of PTSD rather than merely alleviating its symptoms, David Powell's struggle with the past was published only in trauma newsletters and websites for the next fifteen years, until Victor Volkman included "Back Into the Heart of Darkness" in his groundbreaking anthology *Beyond Trauma: Conversations on Traumatic Incident Reduction* (2004). Even now, the accounts of some of the men I interviewed are raising controversy among special interest veteran's groups who, like the "Swiftboaters," want to rewrite military history to conform to their mythology. In the face of this, David has decided to tell his full story—the one he spent decades trying to forget.

The fact that this book is now in your hands speaks volumes about David's extraordinary honesty and bravery. *My Tour in Hell, A Marine's Battle with Combat Trauma* is his sometimes cold-blooded account of thirteen months in Vietnam that had an indelible impact on the rest of his life.

Reading about David's early days as a cocky Kenpo Karate champ all the way through to his painful years of post-war trauma—and yes, unapologetic bias about modes of therapy—I'm particularly proud of him, because I know how difficult it was for David to speak about these things—let alone write about them.

His account comes at a particularly poignant moment in American history, a moment when our country is being led by a Commander in Chief and his cadre of academic ideologues who not only avoided military service—in Vietnam or anywhere else—but have managed to embroil our troops in a quagmire all too reminiscent of the horrors in Southeast Asia, and sell American voters the simplistic promise of "Iraqi Freedom" as if it were a brand of soft drink. Have we really forgotten the lessons of our own history? Walter Cronkite's scathing condemnation of Nixon's "Vietnamization" policy? Country Joe McDonald's "Fish Cheer?"

David Powell has not forgotten the lesson. He will never lose sight of it, or stop pointing it out, and after reading *My Tour in Hell* you'll understand why. Even though our current administration—in the comfort of their armchair chariots—will never have a clue what David means by *semper fidelis*, one can only hope his no-holds-barred candor will be of some solace to the veterans of our current misunderstood, misreported, and misremembered conflict when they come home to its lingering memories.

— Tom Joyce,
January 2006

End Notes

[1] *The Oxford Companion to the Mind*, (Oxford: Oxford University Press, 1987)

[2] Freud, Sigmund, *Two Short Accounts of Psychoanalysis*, (tr.) James Strachey (Singapore: Penguin Books,   1984), p. 37

[3] Nixon, Richard M., *No More Vietnams*   (New York: Avon Books, 1994)

[4] *Information Please Almanac*, (Boston & New York: Houghton Mifflin, 1996)

[5] McCaffrey, Barry R., speech given Memorial Day 1993 at Vietnam Memorial in Washington D.C. [reproduced in *Pentagram*, 4 June 1993]

[6] Combat Area Casualty File [CACF] November 1993, Center for Electronic Records, National Archives,

Washington, D.C.

[7] Ibid. McCaffrey

[8] Ibid. McCaffrey

[9] Figley, Charles R., *Stress Disorders among Vietnam Veterans: Theory, Research and Treatment* (New York: Brunner/Mazel, 1978)

[10] Tiffany, W.J. & Allerton, W.S., "Army Psychiatry in the Mid-60s" (American Journal of Psychiatry, 1967, 123: 810-821)

[11] Bourne, P.G., Men, Stress and Vietnam (Boston: Little, Brown, 1970)

[12] The President's Commission on Mental Health, 1978

[13] HealthCommunities.com

Preface

Are you a survivor of severe trauma? Then this book is for you. I have written this memoir so you can understand my own traumatic experiences in combat and in my life after returning from the killing fields of Vietnam.

I will take you with me through my journey into, through, and out the other side of trauma. I am, and will forever be, a recovering casualty of Post Traumatic Stress Disorder (PTSD[1]). The United States Veterans Administration has rated my disability at 100%, *total and permanent in nature.* The Social Security Administration has also rated my disability at 100%, totally unemployable. I am grateful for these considerations, and I am positive that I retain my creativity, trustworthiness, and good will toward others.

There is closure and healing for us casualties, as my story shows.

I hope you will find the journey interesting, especially if you have not **been there, done that** and wondered what it would have been like to serve your country as a combatant in the chaos and fog of the Vietnam conflict. Although I served just thirteen months in 'Nam during 1966-67, I have seen enough grief, suffering, and atrocity to last a lifetime. I have witnessed the very worst inhumanity that mankind can dish out, a callous disregard for the lives of others and self without limit. It was an environment so heinous that men would set off live hand grenades *against themselves* just to escape its grip. It was only my faith in God that carried me through to the end of my tour in hell.

The next two decades following my return continued to be hellish and painful for me. The personal cost of my disability was immense. Before the war, I had a wife, a decent job, friends, and even a house in the suburbs. After the war, I held as many as eighteen different jobs in the space of ten years and left two different sets of children to grow up without their dad. I was both afraid of my anger and embarrassed by my severe startle reactions, hypervigilance, and lack of emotional control. That's what 100% disability means to me.

---

[1] See the Frequently Asked Questions about PTSD, from the National Center for PTSD, in Appendix B.

In late 1988, I was introduced to a psychological therapy known as Traumatic Incident Reduction, which has vastly improved my mental health and probably saved me from committing suicide... Yes, I was in that much mental anguish. TIR also helped other combat vets I have known personally, including my friend Pieter who had hit rock-bottom, using heroin to self-medicate.

Since therapy, I have discovered a richness in life that is worth embracing. I have found infinite patience and empathy for the travails of others. I have reclaimed my mental health and my self-respect. My self-esteem is strong and growing. I am happy and able to have relationships again.

I believe that many, many others have also experienced traumatic episodes in their lives, and I respect that. This book has been written for those men and women who served their country in battle, have returned with loss of limb, senses, and/or have psychological wounds. It is also written for the people that love them, and is also relevant to anyone who has suffered severe trauma: survivors of criminal assault including rape and domestic violence, or natural disasters, terrorist action, and so on.

Survivors
by Siegfried Sassoon

No doubt they'll soon get well; the shock and strain
Have caused their stammering, disconnected talk.
Of course they're 'longing to go out again,' —
These boys with old, scared faces, learning to walk.
They'll soon forget their haunted nights; their cowed
Subjection to the ghosts of friends who died,—
Their dreams that drip with murder; and they'll be proud
Of glorious war that shatter'd all their pride...
Men who went out to battle, grim and glad;
Children, with eyes that hate you, broken and mad.

Craiglockhart, October 1917

1 Welcome to Hell

Combat is a living hell that can induce profound traumatic stress in veterans. In my opinion, I had more than my share of traumatic experiences. I served in the Marine Corps with Delta Company, 1st Battalion, 7th Marines, of the 1st Marine Division at Chu Lai and Da Nang. Come along with me and I'll tell you some of what I saw and did in 1966 and 1967 in Viet Nam.

I'll also tell you how my life was impacted in very negative ways and how I found help some two decades later.

I was in Chu Lai, South Vietnam, on November 7th, 1966, which was about one month after arriving in country. Ironically, exactly a year from that day I'd leave that hellhole and return to the United States, the country I was proud to serve and protect.

My MOS (Military Occupational Specialty) was 0351, or anti-tank assault man. My primary weapon was the M20 3.5 inch Rocket Launcher. I'd been in country with Delta Company for two weeks but I only knew the last name of my team leader, Jones.

Jones had been in Vietnam five months before me. He was a quiet, down-to-earth black guy. He was a bit taller than me, and he spoke low and softly, like he didn't want anyone to notice him. Jones was concerned about Jones getting home in one piece, and alive. We all had that same goal.

I'd met five other men who lived in the tent I then called home, but I'd forgotten their names at that point.

I was going on my first company-sized *search-and-destroy* mission that day. I'd be in the countryside for the next seven days. I was edgy and afraid of the unknown I was going to know intimately.

I wore my boot camp issued boots, trousers, and shirt. My helmet, flak jacket, rifle, bayonet knife, and backpack were field-worn. I had picked up

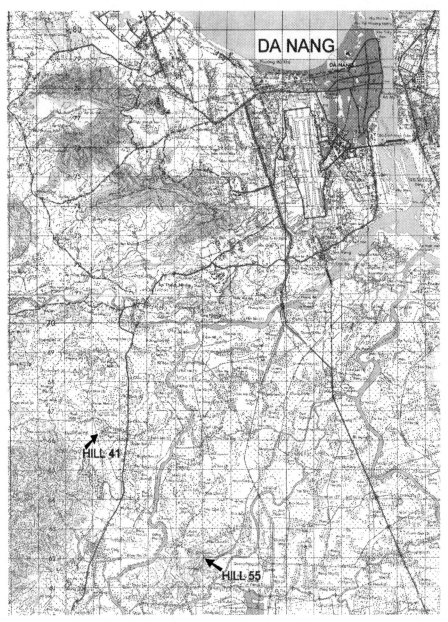

Strategic view of Da Nang and Delta Co. TAORs.
Scale: 1 grid square equals 1 km (0.62 miles)
Map courtesy of USGS.

the older gear as I traveled from the Chu Lai airbase to Delta. I trembled slightly, and my stomach was churning.

When we went out on that size of an operation, we were going well out of our usual area of responsibility into unfamiliar territory. We went where we suspected the VC were building up their strength and preparing to attack us.

We had a Tactical Area of Operational Responsibility (TAOR) we routinely protected. In the center of the TAOR was Hill 41[2] where we stayed, slept, and stood watch. We sent out patrols within our TAOR, and that kept our base relatively safe.

Patrols I participated in were typically comprised of the following: three Riflemen up front, the first of whom was designated "Point man." The designated Patrol Leader followed next, then a Radioman, Corpsman, Machine gunner, his A-Gunner (assistant gunner), Rocket team, and three Riflemen to the rear.

When we ventured outside the TAOR, we went where the VC had their pleasure. They knew they wouldn't be bothered every day, so they took their time and set up sophisticated booby traps, planned and rehearsed ambushes, built bunkers, tunnels, and the like.

This particular combat operation got underway at exactly 3 am on November 7th, 1966. It was a dark morning, no moonlight to see by, and it was raining. We moved out in a single column and headed toward the Phu Long River. A raised road, called a causeway, gave us access to the Villes on the other side of the river (Ville is a French word literally meaning "village"). About an hour into the march, our column snaked over a waist-high fence.

Right at that very moment I had diarrhea. Nerves, I guess, but I thought I could hold myself together 'til we stopped for a break. No such luck! When I straddled the fence I couldn't hold back my urges. Yep! Right down both legs. Until a break came, around 4:30 am, I sloshed along with my pants full of my own feces chapping my thighs. When we

---

[2] See 7th Marines veterans website for a complete list of TAORs (http://www.marzone.com/7thMarines/Mp0001.htm)

stopped, I dropped my pants, cut off my skivvies with my bayonet knife, and threw my polluted shorts in a nearby bush. That made Jones laugh! I quickly added embarrassment on top of my barely concealed nervousness.

We started marching again after a ten-minute break and a cup of coffee. I made the coffee from a C-ration packet and some water from my canteen. Dawn came a couple hours later, about 6 am. The rain had stopped and I could finally see further ahead than Jones' back, clear up the whole column. The last of the company had just finished crossing the river.

I walked along, following Jones, not thinking about anything other than keeping up with the pace of our march with my forty-pound pack on my back.

Suddenly, I was startled back into reality.

We were under attack! The VC (Viet Cong) fired their rifles at us, strafing the whole column. They'd hidden in the brush off to the left of us, and they struck at the midpoint of our column.

I froze! The sound of bullets that came in my direction turned me to stone. My naive twenty-five year old soul heard the air around my head pierced with the flights of bullets that raced by me, followed immediately by the sound of "firecrackers".

I stood still where I was, as rigid as a turkey peering above a fallen tree trunk trying to see the source of the call "gobble, gobble", cackled by hunters who would have had me for dinner. I tasted chalk in my mouth, smelled the jungle plant life I was standing in, felt the cold air blow between my still-wet thighs, and saw nothing around me, though my eyes were wide open and my eyelids refused to blink.

I trembled, ever so slightly, from head to toe. The forty pounds of rockets, C-rations, and other gear in my pack bent me over somewhat. I stood there in a crouch. The enemy fire continued, and I continued standing in place, unable to think or move. My war had begun, and my life as I had known it, ended.

Luckily, a squad member behind me kicked me in my right calf muscle and knocked me back into real life. I dived onto the ground.

"Don't just stand there, you idiot!"

It scared me to think that I'd choked under fire. I was scared, embarrassed, and felt totally alone. This was the first of several other episodes that made me fear and loathe open spaces.

Men, somewhere up the column, returned fire. Then, as quickly as the attack started, it ended. The column moved about three meters to the left, off the trail we were following, and into the trees and undergrowth running alongside it. We resumed heading forward and continued marching another hour or so.

Moving through the bushes and between trees was slow and difficult. When the trees were close together, I had to take off my pack and rocket rounds, turn sideways, and force myself between them, tug my gear through, and then put my stuff back on. I hated having to slow down like that, and even stop sometimes. I kept flashing back to the time I'd been terrified under fire. I felt like a prime target each time I slowed down.

At first, as I struggled to walk through the matted undergrowth, I kicked my feet free when they snagged. Jones noticed what I was doing and punched me in my left shoulder.

"You could set off a booby trap doing that! Stop it! From now on, back your foot out and step over the stuff."

Barely half an hour later, his field smarts proved him right. I heard a muffled explosion somewhere up the column and we came to another stop. Word came down the column, telling us to take cover in place and watch our flanks. A man far ahead of us had detonated a hand-grenade booby trap. A VC was captured nearby the explosion site. Men brought the captive to the rear and into an open field to the left of me.

He was a little squirt, who wore white pajamas, turned filthy, and had short, black hair. He sat in a low squat. All the Vietnamese I saw squatted the same way, resting their butts on their heels, leaning their chests against their overstretched upper thighs.

A fellow Marine stood about three meters in front of the captive, guarding him with a .45 caliber pistol aimed right at his head. The guard was a Staff Sergeant I didn't recognize. He was about five-eleven, over a hundred-eighty pounds, I would've guessed, and his clothing and gear looked new. I got the impression that he was a cocky dude by the way he swaggered around the prisoner.

As I stared at the two of them, I heard another explosion from not very far up the column, and profanities being shouted from that direction. I heard a blood-chilling wail. It was loud, starting out like a throaty groan, and raised in scale and volume to a scream, like a baby being scalded by boiling water. Crying and sobbing followed it. After a few minutes, all was quiet.

I looked back at the VC and saw him laugh quietly to himself.

"Think something's funny?" The guard yelled at the captive, quickly raising his arm, then shot him at point blank range in the forehead with his .45 caliber pistol. He lingered there for a moment as if to torment the captive.

That was my first *slow motion picture* experience. By that I mean my world seemed to move forward, frame-by-frame, in my mind's-eye, clearly showing me all the details of what I was seeing. That time I saw the bullet enter the captive's forehead, then exit the back of his skull, and the kicked up mud as the bullet hit the ground behind him.

Blood gushed out the front of his head, more out of the back of his head, with some skull fragments. The VC silently slumped to the ground, landed on his left side and remained there, motionless. The guard and another man slung his body into a nearby hedge. My life shifted back into present time and the *slow motion recording* ended. I was in Vietnam, trying to save my life and my mind.

I'd just witnessed my first murder, in cold blood! I was shocked and disgusted. That was the first time I'd watched men act so mercilessly, with no remorse, inflicting pain, suffering and death on the people I thought I was here to save from Communist oppression. Unfortunately, it wouldn't be the last time I saw such things. It was, however, a memory I never wanted, and lived with since that day.

Almost immediately, a Captain approached the guard.

"What happened here?"

"Sir! He tried to escape!"

The Captain turned away, obviously disgusted, and muttered, "Carry on". He hadn't even asked where the body was, let alone attempted to verify the Sergeant's claim.

The Officer in charge of our operation called for a Medevac. A Medivac is an abbreviation for 'Medical Evacuation'. Someone radios headquarters and asks for a helicopter to come and pick up our wounded and/or dead men. A chopper would come in and airlift the victim(s) back to the rear for emergency treatment. On that occasion, both wounded men were helped into a "Huey" UH-1 chopper.

Typical UH-1 Medevac operation (10/16/1969). Source: Nat'l Archives

We waited there another 15 minutes for the Medevac. As the chopper took off, we began marching again. I walked maybe another hundred meters and discovered a hideously grotesque scene. At first it appeared to be a backpack lying on its side near a tree.

I leaned over to look at it. It was a combat boot, not a pack, and it had a human's foot inside it, with the lower part of a leg protruding out. The wail I heard must have come from here, I figured.

I saw the shinbone, white and splintered, sticking out of the boot. About half an inch above that was bloody, burned flesh.

So this is what a grenade can do to people, I thought.

I gagged and shook; I was so sickened at the sight. The coffee I'd drank while we were on our break, along with some stomach bile, made its way back into my throat. I re-swallowed it. I imagined myself suffering a terrible wound such as that and felt deeply sorry for the poor man who was now disabled, and sorry for myself because that could happen to me, too.

As I looked around the area, I could see that this was indeed where one of the Medivac'ed men had been wounded. I left his boot in the hedge. I shut my mouth tight and continued marching. I was afraid that if I pointed it out to anyone else, I'd be stuck carrying it until we stopped again.

After a full day's march, dusk finally came and we halted for the night. Jones and I traded turns sleeping and standing watch until the next morning. We followed that routine every night we were on an operation. Jones always took the first watch and I took the second one. That way he made certain he would have an uninterrupted night's sleep. I deeply resented him for that.

Oh, I remember, "Watch!"

When we were back on our hill, "Watch" was slightly different. It lasted three hours at a time, and rotated every evening. That meant I wouldn't always stand watch from 8 to 11 pm. I would stand from 5 to 8 pm the first night, then the next night 8 to 11 pm, and so on throughout the night. I stood watch alone.

I went out to our bunker, near our tent/home and sat there as I stared into the darkness, and fought to stay awake. I looked at my wristwatch every few minutes until the three hours were up.

One particularly starless night I mused about my living quarters. *This is my home, huh?*

My home sat on the side of a hill. The view of the countryside was unobstructed. There were rice paddies all over the valley floor, with rows of trees that marked their boundaries. Where there weren't trees, there were earthen dams. It looked like a "checkerboard" with all of the squares green and wet.

What land wasn't used for rice paddies was thick jungle foliage and elephant grass that grew as high as seven or eight feet. A large river, called the Phu Long, cut straight through the valley to the left of the company hill.

Home was nothing more than a faded green, canvas tent. It held six men, their cots, and provided a hallway that ran from the front door to the back. Three ten-foot posts held up the roof that sloped down on either side. Four six-foot poles, one in each corner, formed the walls. Canvas flaps were called the front and back doors. Sandbags, which we hoped would protect us against enemy fire, were stacked up about four feet high around the tent. The floor was made up of wooden shipping pallets to keep everything above the mud when it rained. That was home.

Drying out the M20 rocket launcher on a sunny day outside my tent.
Source: DWP

I thought about my Pasadena, California home, some 7,827 miles from Chu Lai, though it might as well have been a million or two. My heart and sanity are there, but I'm *not home*. Oh, how I miss being a happy man whose mind isn't stained with the ugly truth that I could very well die out here in this godforsaken land. I'm supposed to fight a life-or-death struggle here just preserve it for the benefit of the South Vietnamese. I'd give anything to be back home right now.

I fought back against grief to visualize it as exactly as I could. It was small, but no smaller than the other nineteen houses on either side of the street. It was about eleven hundred square feet, overall. The attached garage was to the left of the front door, as you faced the house from the street. There was a multi-paned window, about four-by-six feet, to the right of the front door.

It had a stucco exterior. The inside walls were painted eggshell white. The floors were carpeted, wall-to-wall. The kitchen and bathroom had white linoleum floors. There was one bathroom with a tub and shower setup and a one-person sink with a mirrored medicine cabinet above it. The larger one of the two bedrooms was my wife's, and mine and the other was designated as the guest room. That was my *real home.*

The worst watch for me was always the last one, which started at 5 am. It was supposed to last three hours, but I never figured out when it really ended. Those days became one long session of watching for the VC. My vigil never ended, it would seem.

When watch was over, I returned to the tent. I lightly touched the outstretched foot of the man who followed my watch. He often woke with a start. We said nothing to one another. He went out the back door to the bunker. I crawled into my cot and went back to sleep. Even if the base was not home, it was better than where I was, out on patrol.

On the second day of the operation, November 8th, 1966, in midafternoon, the front of the column came under heavy enemy fire. The command "Rockets!" came down the column.

Whenever we came under fire, everybody got down as low to the ground as possible. But, in order to respond to the order "Rockets," the team had to get up and run to the point of attack. In this case, Jones and I ran up the line. The Rocket Gunner carried the rocket launcher. The A-Gunner carried additional rockets for the launcher.

Jones and I quickly trotted to the front of the line, where we were taking enemy rifle fire. Ahead of us, lying prone on the ground, were three men, frantically pointing at a cluster of trees about a hundred meters in front of their position.

"See them trees they're pointing at, Powell?"

"Yeah, Jones, I see them."

"You take the launcher. There's a WP [White Phosphorous] round in the launcher. Shoot it right where I'm pointing. If it hits close enough, it'll burn 'em. Anyways, there'll be enough smoke so Arty can call in a fire mission." ('Arty' is short for Artillery)

"I know what'll happen, man. Don't treat me like I'm stupid. Just tap my helmet when the rocket's armed!"

Disassembled M-20 still on his lap, a Marine enjoys a smoke after a daylight raid, Nevada Cities area, (Korea) 1953. Source: Nat'l Archives

There were three main ways I knew to fire a launcher. I could stand upright, but that made me an easy target. I could kneel to the ground on one leg, which was my favorite position, or I could lie prone on the ground. If I were lying prone, I had to make sure my outstretched legs wouldn't get hit with the rocket's back blast.[3]

Marine Corps enlistees train with M20 bazookas at Camp Matthews, La Jolla, CA (early 1950s). Source: Nat'l Archives

I knelt, took aim, and waited for Jones' tap. I could barely feel the arming switch rise on the launcher. Right after that, I felt Jones thump on my head and heard him scurry for cover off to my left. I squeezed the trigger, but all I heard was a loud click and a low sizzling noise in my right ear. The electrically triggered rocket had misfired!

---

[3] The "Zone A" blast area (up to 25 yards *behind* the M20), should be clear of all personnel, ammunition, materiel, and flammables, such as dry vegetation. The danger in this area is from the blast of flame to the rear of the launcher and the rearward flight of nozzle closures and/or igniter wires. (TM 9-1055-201-12, M20A1 *Operator's Manual*)

I looked at Jones. He stared back at me, and his eyes seemed as big as baseballs.

Jones yelled, "Hang Fire!"

I'm sure anyone within fifty meters of him heard his scream. Man, was he ever in a state of panic.

"Hang Fire" meant that the rocket was armed, stuck in the tube, and could explode at any minute.

Jones, and every man who heard him, got up from their positions and ran away from me, leaving me alone and in the open.

I'm going to die, I thought. I crouched there, waiting for the rocket to explode. Minutes, which seem like hours, slowly ticked off. Where are the men who should have been by my side at a time like this? I was both embittered and scared out of my mind!

Eventually, Jones came back and grasped the tube so I could stand. I took it back from him and carefully laid it in a nearby trench. I threw my flak jacket over the firing end of the tube, then rolled a hand grenade down the front of the tube and ducked for cover. The grenade went off and the rocket exploded. My flak jacket smothered the explosion.

That was the only way I could think of to disarm the launcher. I hadn't been taught what to do if something like that ever happened. If it had been a High Explosive round, the launcher would surely have been totaled. But although WP burns hot, it's not technically an explosive.

I shouted, "All Clear!"

Jones pulled the launcher out of the trench, put in another round, and ordered me to fire again. I knew that to disobey a direct order would mean an eventual court-martial. Somehow (don't ask me how) I fought through my fears and fired it. It worked fine. Within minutes artillery rounds were raining all over the hill where my rocket landed. The enemy attacks stopped. I knew (then) that at least one thing was certain: *I'm the only one that's going to get me through this tour alive!* That conclusion proved to be a long-lasting one, indeed.

Until a few years ago, I had trouble trusting anyone who has/had even a modicum of authority over me. Further, my fear of abandonment was

compounded. Lying alongside that emotion was my hatred of being "ordered" to do things I didn't want to do, yet having to do them,
embarrassment at my combat ineptitude, and fear of open spaces.

When we needed munitions, food or other supplies, we'd let the company commander know what we needed and we'd get re-supplied. Supply
would send our stuff to us by helicopter. If the area where we set up a de-
fensive perimeter seemed safe to land, they'd come down and offload our
supplies. If the area were dangerous, they'd fly low over us and dropped it
near us.

I showed Jones that my boot camp issued footgear was rotting off my
feet.

"Can I get another pair of boots?"

"Sure. I'll tell the Lieutenant and he'll phone it in. You look pretty
stupid in those stateside boots, anyways!"

My new jungle boots eventually arrived along with a set of jungle utili-
ties (camouflage cotton fatigues), a new flak jacket, C-rations, and rocket
rounds. The jungle boots were made of leather and canvas, with rein-
forced soles, to protect our feet from Punji stakes.

Punji stakes were bamboo stalks, about a foot long, sharpened to a
point on one end. The VC stuck them in the ground, pointed end up,
hoping we would step, or fall, on them.

On this operation, we marched around for another two or three days,
but fortunately we didn't make any more enemy contact. We began heading back to our hill, by way of the Red Sea shoreline. Mid-morning came,
and the sun shone brightly. I was hot, tired, sweating, and had already seen
all the combat I cared to see for the rest of my life. I was angry at the
world!

"Why the heck do we have to march in the sand, under the glare of
this sun? Where's our cover!"

"Just be glad we're going home, Powell," Jones said.

I was with a squad that was about a hundred men following the Point
man.

Point man signals "danger ahead" on a patrol. Source: DWP

In my opinion, "Point man" was the worst possible position to have on a patrol. "Point" led the way. He was the first to step through tree lines, which were sometimes set up with trip-wired grenades. He was the first to enter clearings, which made him an obvious target. "Point" had to protect the advancement of the rest of the men.

The front of the column had just turned inland from the beach. They had come under fire from an ambush along the trail they were taking back to our respective hills. I rushed off to my right, reaching the top of a sand dune that overlooked the point of attack.

The VC who attacked us ran from their tree line position and retreated down into rice paddies. They were about three hundred meters away from my position. There were fifty-some men lying side by side along the dune, firing down at the escaping enemy, but I was up there in a world of my own. I waited for an opportunity to sight in on one of attackers. I aimed slightly ahead of the one I'd picked out, and fired. It was a fabulous shot!

The VC fell to his knees and I shot him two more times before he fell off the dike and splashed into the paddy.

"I got one of them, right where you're standing, to the left of you!" I shouted down to a man who was chasing the attackers.

I was elated! My heart was pounding heavily, and I had a grin on my face that threatened to rip my cheeks apart. I had done my job and maybe saved some lives for our side!

The man I shouted at found the body and called two other men to help drag the victim back to the inland trail.

As we resumed our march home again, I passed by my first kill, lying to the right of the trail. A Corpsman from another platoon knelt over the body, trying to see if there was anything he could do to save his life. I saw that one of my bullets had torn through both thighs of the VC. Another bullet had entered the left side of the chest, and the last one slammed into the right buttocks. My victim was slender, pale-skinned, and about five-five in height, or length in that case. There was blood everywhere. I was shocked and mortified.

"That's my hit, Doc!", I blurted out.

I felt confused when Doc gave me a dirty look. The disdain and hate for me that was filling his eyes said it all.

I bent over the body to get a closer look. The "He" I thought I'd shot turned out to be a "She". I pretended it didn't matter to me, but it did... I was filled with remorse. I looked down so others wouldn't see the tears that suddenly filled my eyes. My breathing turned into short gasps of air and my mouth became dry. The water I drank from my canteen didn't help my condition. I fell back in line and resumed the march homeward. I suddenly thought of myself as a killer, not a soldier.

We moved only another fifty meters, or so, and we got ambushed again. I immediately dived to the ground. *Quite a different reaction than the first time I had been shot at*, I reflected.

I fell face down, and broke my fall with the butt-end of my M14 rifle. I buried the butt-end in the soft dirt and sand I landed in at the side of the trail. I aimed and tried to fire my rifle toward where I thought the VCs were. My rifle was jammed!

I took the magazine out and saw I still had bullets. I tried to pull the bolt back to see if a cartridge was stuck in the barrel, but the bolt was rock-solid shut and wouldn't budge. When the butt of my rifle hit the ground, sand and dirt had flown into the breech.

I heard bullets fly over my head, so I rolled over a couple times to my left, and clutched my rifle to my chest.

I put the rifle between my knees, butt to the ground, and tried to stomp the bolt open. It didn't budge. After the attack ended, we continued back toward our hills. I was essentially unarmed.

I felt rattled and scared. Now I was a walking, talking target. I felt like I weighed three hundred pounds, stood seven feet tall, and was as obvious a target as a white barn in the middle of a green pasture.

Luckily, we all got back to our hills without further incidents. I found my way back to my tent, shed my pack, rocket rounds and rifle, then sat on my cot and leaned forward, and stared at the floor.

I began to cry, silently, but shed no tears. I forced air into and out of my lungs because I couldn't breathe normally. I reflected on my recent experiences; I was nearly wounded (or killed) by rifle fire, had avoided booby traps, saw what the traps could do to people, had my rocket launcher misfire, was abandoned by my *comrades* while under enemy fire, killed a human being, and had my rifle jam and become inoperable.

I felt a multitude of emotions. I'd faced my mortality and was frightened to death of it. I knew what fear felt like, how it tasted and smelt, and what it looked like on the faces of others. I witnessed a callous murder and abhorred the experience. I had become a murderer, myself.

After that operation, I wanted desperately to go home. That was impossible to do. I was to go on at least six more operations of that size or greater, and over a hundred and fifty patrols.

I learned more valuable lessons on my first operation. One: Don't shoot 'til you see something to shoot at, 'cause it'll give away your position. Two: Keep your weapons ready to fire, no matter what else you do.

After about ten minutes on my cot, I returned to normal, physically. My crying spell abated, I breathed normally, and I thanked God for having spared my life and limbs.

I tidied up my *bedroom*. I cleaned my rifle for over an hour, and got it working again. I spent at least an hour on my rifle after each patrol after that first episode, which was way more than anyone else did with their gear. I got the nickname "Lone Ranger," because my barrel shone like silver from my overzealous cleaning.

On a boring, humid day after my first operation, as I polished my rifle, I recalled my first few days at Delta. I'd arrived at dusk. I was soaking wet, and so was all my gear. I was shown an empty cot in my assigned tent and put my stuff down. I tried to sleep, but swarms of mosquitoes flew all around me.

I hate mosquitoes! They had lots of them in 'Nam. That first night was absolutely maddening. I was alone, in the dark, in Viet Nam, with thirteen months ahead of me, and mosquitoes were constantly biting me. There seemed no way I could get to sleep.

Finally, I pulled a blanket up over my head and left one arm exposed. In the morning I woke up with about eighty mosquito bites on that arm.

The other fellows in my tent began moving around at about 5 am. They were all white men. The racial mix of combat men, in my experience, was that about ten percent of them were African-American.

The first man I met was Sergeant Tom Mizell, a squad leader. He had sandy colored hair and brown eyes. I would learn to count on him for any support I needed. He was a tall guy, around six-two, and fifteen pounds underweight. For that matter, they all looked like they had lost considerable weight.

Tom introduced me to Mack and the others. Mack was a Corporal and a machine gunner. He called Kentucky home and his accent confirmed that he was a Southerner. His hair was dark brown and he looked like he hadn't shaved for a couple of days. I later came to find out that he was land-rich. His father had recently passed on and left him acres and acres of land. His grandfather homesteaded the land many years before.

Jimmy was a baby-faced kid from the Midwest. He had light brown hair and blue eyes. He was a machine gunner, too.

Sergeant Tom Mizell. Photo: DWP

Andy was an A-gunner, who teamed with Jimmy. Chicago was his hometown. From the get-go he was a wise-mouthed Italian, with shiny black hair and deep brown eyes. He thought he knew *something* about *everything.*

Henry rounded out the tent family I'd joined. He was a rifleman. He came from New York, and was a very quiet type. His red hair shimmered like a small bonfire. He kept pretty much to himself.

My first words to Tom, after the brief introductions were over were brief and to the point: "I'm Powell. My MOS is 0351. Who's my squad leader?"

"Corporal Jones, but he sleeps in another tent. I'll tell him you're over here."

As I started settling in, Jones came by to meet me.

"I'm Corporal Jones. Let's walk up to the mess hall and I'll fill you in on the routine here."

Jones described what our daily pattern would be like. We'd go on at least one patrol together every day. Since he outranked me, I was to be his A-Gunner. I'd lug as many spare rocket rounds as I could carry and follow behind him, with my rifle.

"We got more patrols than the other grunts, 'cause there's not enough rocket teams for each squad. We'll be supporting several other units that don't have their own rockets."

A Corpsman was having breakfast at the next table. He looked like a Corpsman! His face was angelic, with soft, light blue eyes, no sign of a beard, and was about twenty years old. He was not your rugged, combat stereotype. I told him about my mosquito problem from the night before.

"They ate me alive, Doc!" I showed him my bitten-up arm.

He gave me a bottle of repellent from a bag he carried. I doused myself with some of it. It stung, but it relieved the itch. I made it a routine to always have repellent with me from then on.

Jones and I finished eating and went our separate ways. Back in my tent, I thought about mealtime in 'Nam and how I was going to get nourishment.

The chow from the mess hall was terrible. At breakfast, they served scrambled eggs. They poured a two-cup blob of beaten eggs onto a large griddle, scraped it a couple of times into a mound, then spread it out again with the edge of a food tray. When they served them to us, they were chewy and had a green tinge. The sausages were cold and overcooked, and the toast was either burnt or not warm enough to melt butter.

Lunch was ham and cheese sandwiches, peanut butter sandwiches, or something they called chili and beans. The ham was cut too thinly to taste like ham, the peanut butter was runny, and the chili and beans was more like spiced gravy and lukewarm kidney beans.

Dinner was a choice of meat loaf, sliced roast beef, or sliced turkey, served with mashed potatoes and some mystery vegetable on the side.

I washed down what little food I could chew and swallow with copious amounts of milk or coffee. The chow never improved all the time I was in country.

After sampling the mess hall grub, I preferred eating C-rations to the "food" they provided. C-ration (short for "combat ration") food was something to get used to, all right, but at least it was consistent. At least there were choices I could make about what I'd eat. I had 'heat tabs' I'd burn in a C-ration 'stove' to heat my food over, and the packaged meal was a balanced one, nutritionally speaking, of 1200 calories. Each ration consisted of a canned entree, a "B2 unit" containing cheese, crackers and candy, a canned dessert, and an accessory pack. The accessory pack contained a P-38 can opener, mix for a hot beverage, salt and sugar packets, plastic spoon, chewing gum, a pack of four cigarettes and several sheets of toilet paper.[4]

I finished cleaning my rifle, wrote a letter to my folks, and let the memory of my first days at Delta fade back into my subconscious.

---

[4] Source: Wikipedia (http://en.wikipedia.org/wiki/C-ration)

2 Operation Rio Blanco

"He crouched and flinched, dizzy with galloping fear,
Sick for escape,— loathing the strangled horror
And butchered, frantic gestures of the dead."
— From "Counter-Attack" by Siegfried Sassoon

I had been on another dozen patrols when word came down that we were going on another operation. This one was far, far away from our area. We'd be taking choppers to the battlefield. This incident I believe to have happened as part of Operation Rio Blanco, which went on from November 20th to 27th, 1967, right through Thanksgiving. The 7th Marines were 17 kilometers due West of Quang Ngai city on the Son Tra Khoc river. On November 25, 1966 the 1st Battalion, 7th Marines put three companies on line by helicopter airlift and engaged the VietCong.[5] Delta company was along for the fight.

According to renowned Vietnam author Bill McDonald, who served in Vietnam from 1966 to 1967 as a crew chief/ door-gunner on UH-1D helicopters with the 128th Assault Helicopter Company, over 12,000 helicopters saw action in Vietnam. Of that number, a total of 2,246 helicopters were shot down between the years of 1962 and 1973, and an additional 2,075 were considered operational losses. Being in a helicopter was always dangerous and sometimes a deadly proposition.

Jones and I were attached to a squad. Our company boarded sixteen CH-46 choppers and we flew off. Each helicopter nominally contained a crew of four and up to 22 ground assault troops. We must have flown for at least an hour, so we were at least another fifty miles into the countryside. I peeked up a few times during the flight to look at the rest of the men. Everyone stared at the floor, their faces expressionless. Eventually,.

---

[5] Information based on the account of Ron ("Doc") Ferrel, 1st Battalion, 5th Marines (http://www.marzone.com/corpsman/RF-11.htm).

Bravo Company, 1st Battalion, 7th Marines load into Crew/Chief Joe Silveira's (HMM-165) CH-46 aircraft for movement to a new LZ on Operation Rio Blanco (Nov. 1966). Source: Nat'l Archives

we got to the site of the battle. In series of threes, the choppers landed, men scrambled for cover, and set up fighting positions

When our turn came to land, the tailgate lowered. To the left of our probable landing site I saw another chopper that had been shot up pretty bad. Its engine was spewing flames and smoke. The pilot tried to lift off, but his chopper sunk into the mud and sputtered to a stop. The chopper pilot and crew quickly abandoned ship and ran for cover with our men.

As we descended, I heard a couple of bullets pierce the skin of our chopper. We hovered three or four feet above a rice paddy. All the men jumped out the back and ran for cover, except me. I was last man in line to go. I had started down the tailgate, but my pilot panicked. I deduced he probably thought he was going to be shot down, too.

He suddenly lifted up about thirty feet before I reached the end of the tailgate. A chopper crewman hollered to the pilot that I was still onboard. The chopper quit climbing and hovered for a few seconds. Here was another "slo-mo" episode I endured.

I can't leave Jones down there without his A-Gunner! I'll have to jump!

I had my pack on, with a few days' supply of C-rations, and a rocket pack with three eight-pound rockets attached. I must've been carrying at least forty pounds of gear. I was scared to death! The distance to the ground from where I had to jump was still over thirty feet. I was a fairly good swimming pool diver off a three-meter board, but nothing in my prior life had prepared me for a jump such as that.

I drew in a lungful of air, and then dived off the tailgate. My testes drew back into my lower abdomen. Foot by foot I watched the ground get closer. The further I fell the faster I went, the more horrific the experience became. I belly-flopped into the rice paddy. It was wet and very muddy. Fortunately, the mud cushioned my fall or I might have easily broken a leg or worse. I developed an intense fear of heights as a result of that jump.

Bullets were flying everywhere. I caught up with, and then followed Jones' every move as we made our way to the main part of the company. As we passed by, I couldn't help but notice some of our dead and dying.

It was grimmer than anything I'd ever seen in the movies, or on TV. There was blood weeping from my comrades' wounds, moaning and crying from I knew not where, and my adrenalin flooded my veins and arteries.

This operation was bigger than I had imagined. Instead of just my company there, there were actually three companies fighting that action. Marines were everywhere, and so were the VC. The smell of gun smoke was stifling. The sound of guns firing was deafening.

When I came under fire and rounds seemed to come at me from every direction, I either had what I call "tunnel vision" or I had "horizon vision".

I had "tunnel vision" when I felt I knew where the enemy was firing. I focused on the terrain immediately around the source of the attack. I squinted my eyes, looking for the telltale smoke from a just-fired rifle. It seemed like I looked through binoculars. The times I had "horizon vision," I forced my eyes as wide open as I could, and took in as much of the whole area as I could. That seemed like I was looking at an IMAX movie screen.

Incoming rounds flew from every direction. I caught a glimpse of somebody out of the corner of my eye, to the right of me. He was about twenty meters away. I turned to look directly at him and immediately recognized him. He was the Priest from Regimental HQ I'd met while I traveled to Delta for the first time.

He knelt over a gravely wounded man who lay on the ground in front of him. The Priest took off his helmet with his right hand and laid it beside him. His left hand clutched a rosary and some vestment.

He put his hands together in front of him, and prayed over the chest of the dying man. As he was giving what small comfort of last rites he could, he caught one directly in his temple and fell over to the left. He lay there, motionless. A Corpsman ran over to him, in a crouched position. He shook the priest by his shoulder a couple of times, then "Doc" shook his head "No", as he stared at the ground. "Doc" then fled back into the lines from where he had come. I believed the Priest went straight to Heaven!

This was no good time to let myself become distracted. I filed the memory of that scene in the recesses of my mind. We began working our way into position, readying for our three-company assault. There was a "Master Plan" to the battle at hand that sounded good but was seriously flawed.

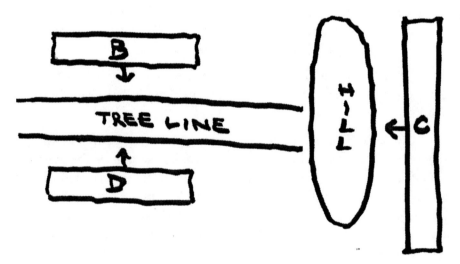

Operation Rio Blanco battle orders

I've drawn you a crude picture of a piece of landscape where the "brilliant" battle I participated in was planned and executed. The oblong circle near the far edge represents a fairly high hill. The two lines that come from the hill, across the middle are supposed to indicate a tree line. Behind the hill, on the edge of the paper, I drew a rectangle with a C, for Charlie Company.

That's where they were dropped in, by helicopter. Above the tree line is another rectangle; Bravo Company was positioned there. The rectangle below the tree line is where Delta Company, my unit, set up. The plan was to have Charlie company advance up the hill and drive the VC down into this tree line, where we would ambush them.

We formed up into a column and began working our way along a tree line. Word came down the line that Charlie company was chasing about a hundred VC off of the hill, into the tree line about fifty meters in front of our position. Jones and I set up behind a dike and aimed the launcher at the trees. When he said he was ready, I yelled "Back blast!", which meant that a rocket was about to be fired.

The men who came up behind us took cover. Jones fired. The back blast spewed gas and shards of wiring out of the breach. I once caught a tiny bit of blue wire in my right eyelid. It stayed embedded there for years.

The order "Get On Line!" came down to us. That, to me, was another one of the worst commands I had to obey. "Get on Line." Imagine a line of fifty or more men standing shoulder-to-shoulder on the sideline of a football field. They face the other sideline. The enemy is on the other sideline.

"Forward!" The command to attack was announced. I took a quick, deep breath and held it.

Please, God, don't let me die!

As ordered, we held our rifles hip-high, and fired repeatedly as we marched directly at the enemy.

Charlie company accomplished exactly what they had intended to do. The VC ran off the hill and into the tree line to escape. When we advanced against the enemy, so would Bravo. In other words, the VC would be caught in between Bravo and Delta, and our two companies would be shooting at the VC, but we were also shooting at each other. The problem was obvious! Either Bravo or Delta should have advanced toward the tree line, but not both of them at the same time!

I walked and fired straight ahead, at the same pace as the others. I was spared, but in my peripheral vision I could see men drop, wounded or dead, to the ground. The gunfire drowned out their screams, if in fact they did scream. The gunfire noise from 10 men simultaneously firing M14s, repeatedly and constantly, deafened me.

When I entered the tree line I saw at least a dozen VC lying on the ground, pretty shot up. I watched, in disgust, as Private Dewey, a rifleman I had been on a few patrols with put his foot on the chest of a dead VC.

Dewey was shorter than most of us. He acted like he had a chip on his shoulder. He held his rifle in his right hand and his helmet was cocked to one side. He held his left hand up in a fist and stomped on the dead VC's chest. Blood squirted out through the bullet holes like a miniature garden fountain. I couldn't force myself to look away; some hideous part of me wanted to watch this macabre act.

"YEEHAW," he screeched.

I was sickened and nauseated by the scene, and ashamed to have been one of the "Lookie Loo's."

Back home, after the battle, Delta learned that we shot up Bravo pretty bad. After that our company was nicknamed "Deadly Delta."

•   •   •

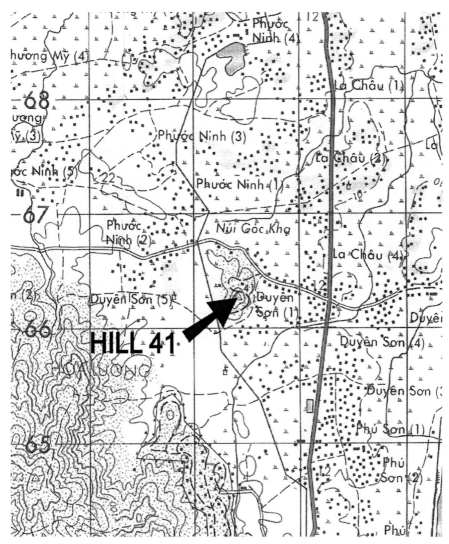

Hill 41 TAOR. Map courtesy USGS (Map 6640-IV, coords AT 934664)

Taking a break in the Ville. Source: DWP

Patrols back on Hill 41 had become commonplace. We rarely were shot at and the booby traps the VC set for us were amateurish and fairly easy to spot. I thought that the VC waited for us to become lazy on patrol, then they would surprise us.

Once, when we took a break at a Ville, I left the other men, who were screwing around with the villagers in their huts, and stood watch under a shady tree. I sat on a rock, daydreaming about being back in America, when a VC took a potshot at me. The dreaming stopped! I fell to one side and got ready to fire. The other men scrambled out of the huts and looked like the "Keystone Cops," from a scene out of an old black-and-white film. They ran around in all directions. If it wasn't real life, it could have been funny. I was mad at myself for letting my guard down. It was never safe to forget where you were and what you were doing.

•   •   •

VC wrapped in duct tape, found deceased. Source: DWP

On another operation in the Phu Longs across the river, the front of the line came under fire. A VC, whose whole upper body was wrapped in duct tape, had been shot and killed. The tape was not there for protection. Rather, his idea was if he got shot he could continue his charge at us because the bullet(s) would pierce straight through his chest. He knew he was going to die and he wanted to take as many of us with him as he could, before he himself had been shot and killed.

The column came to a stop and we took a fifteen-minute break. I saw his body off the trail to my right. I sat on top of a large rock and looked around my area for anything dangerous.

Two men decided to pull the body onto the trail. They then proceeded to crush the man's skull with a large rock. They took turns with each other until they succeeded.

They both emitted the now-familiar squeal ("YEEHAW") as the man's brain matter oozed onto the ground.

"For heaven's sake, guys! Knock it off. You're grossing me out!"

I looked away in disgust. Now I had come to know that even the dead were disrespected.

I fight alongside murderers and mutilators. Will I become like them? I pray to God that day that He would spare me those sins.

I faced back down the column, to my rear. I spotted three VC trotting away. I could tell they were VC because they were young men, wore black pajama outfits, and were obviously hurrying away from any confrontation with our outfit.

I immediately jumped from the rock, took aim, and fired at them. I hit one of them and grazed another. The two still standing tried to drag their fallen friend along with them, but my shots at them made them forget their plan. They ran away, full speed and escaped. The Marines near where I shot the man confirmed that he was dead. They did so by turning their attention back to their C-ration lunch, and left the VC on the ground where they found him.

That was kill number two for me.

My soul felt scarred.

I believed that I was fighting in Viet Nam to free the South Vietnamese from the North Vietnamese. I had justified to myself that if I had to kill people in combat, then so be it. I had killed twice now. Each one I killed was during a combat setting, but my personal safety was not in jeopardy either time. So, truthfully, it wasn't a question of "kill or be killed".

I thought of myself as a very faithful Christian. "Thou shall not kill" meant a lot to me. Nonetheless, I had killed people.

From now on, I was determined to only fire at others when my life or my comrades' lives were threatened, I swore to The Almighty.

On or around early December 1966, Lance Corporal Hobarth was hit by a waist-high grenade booby trap. It filled his groin with shrapnel and he was Medivac'ed all the way to Okinawa for treatment.

Hobarth was another rocket gunner in our squad. All he ever ate, like me, was C-rations, and was probably twenty pounds below what he should have weighed. He rarely spoke, and when he did he usually had to be asked to repeat himself in order to be understood.

I was meritoriously promoted to Lance Corporal and took over Hobarth's launcher.

3 The New Guy

New guys were dangerous. That's why I didn't get close to them. They froze up in combat, just like I did the first time I was attacked.

Somebody standing up draws attention to themselves. Consequently, there were more bullets headed in the direction of the New Guy. If you were near the New Guy you were at a greater risk of being hit.

New Guys were clumsy—they'd trip the fish-wired hand grenade booby traps. They'd step on the buried mortar rounds. When someone got wounded, it stopped the whole mission. We stopped and tended to them and helped them any way we could. In the case of larger mines and booby traps, I could get hit by some of the stuff that didn't hit the New Guy. I'd be wounded even if I were not at fault.

"Short-Timers" were also dangerous. A Short Timer was anybody who had about thirty days left on his tour. It was my experience that "short timing" kicked in about three months before their rotation stateside.

Short Timers refused to go out on patrol. If I insisted they go, as I had to do, I ran the risk that the guy would shoot me. Alternatively, he could throw a hand grenade in a bush next to where I stood and then say, "Oh, too bad. He must've hit a booby trap." I had no real authority over them, but I felt it was my responsibility to the other guys to make sure that patrols were properly manned.

The Short Timer was afraid because he knew what could happen to him. The New Guy was afraid because he *didn't know* what could happen to him.

A new man to the platoon, named Walker, became my A-Gunner. I was not at all thrilled to be the one who broke in a new man.

Walker was barely eighteen. He was four or five inches shorter than me. His hair was sandy blond and he was a little pudgy around his waist. He acted scared of everybody and everything. As it would soon turn out, his behavior nearly put me in a body bag on more than one occasion.

Heading out on a patrol from Hill 41 toward the Phu Long river (March 1967). Source: DWP

I took Walker out on six or seven patrols in the safer areas around the hill. He was very wary at first and I knew to expect that of him. I didn't expect him to remain overly wary after he got used to being in the field, but he did.

I had to constantly tell him what to do, and what not to do. My frustration grew each time I had to tell him the same things, over and over again. Frankly, my frustration with him turned into anger and distrust.

We went on another company-sized operation in the Phu Longs. It was Walker's first operation, and we left before dawn, as usual. It was very dark, but the stars gave off enough light for me to see the riflemen walking in front of me, at a distance of about three meters.

Walker crept slowly behind me. He walked so slowly that I had to order him to pick up his pace every six or seven steps. I was gradually losing sight of the man I was following and I began feeling pretty anxious. Finally, I stopped marching, turned around to face Walker, and took his face in my hand, gripping his chin.

"Either keep up with me from now on, or I'm going to get you transferred out of my team when we get back to the hill!" I growled.

I turned back around, and discovered that I had lost contact with the rest of the column. A horrible feeling crept into my mind, up from my stomach. I had now become de facto "Point" for the fifty-plus men following me.

I believed "Point man" was the worst possible position to have on a patrol. I was armed with all the wrong weapons for the job that had now fallen on my shoulders. I shuddered at the thought and my bladder involuntarily emptied.

I had no choice but to move forward. My awareness of the surroundings was now heightened to the max. I cradled the launcher between my forearms and biceps, drew and cocked my pistol, and began to lead the rest of the men.

I stepped forward very slowly, expecting a land mine to explode each time I shifted my weight onto every forward step I took. I tried to look everywhere at the same time. I was completely ill-prepared for the role I had been forced into.

I began to approach a barely visible tree line and heard the sound of shuffling feet on the other side of the trees, in a small clearing. I saw the shadows of three men standing there. I took my pistol and pointed it directly at the figures. For some quirky reason I said, "Halt! Who goes there?" instead of immediately opening fire on them.

"I'm Point for Bravo Company."

Oh, what a fatal mistake I had narrowly avoided. I dropped the barrel of my pistol down to my side. A few more steps forward brought me in contact with the man I had originally been following. The column had stopped for a break and I was able to reconnect with the rest of the company.

We'd been out for three days when we approached the other causeway that crossed the Phu Long River, leading back to our side of the terrain. I was on high ground looking down at the river. The men below, along the riverbank, came under fire from a daylight ambush. I spotted some VC in a canoe rowing away from the skirmish. They were about four hundred meters away and I could see their rifles lying on their laps.

An artillery barrage was called in on them. In their panic, they capsized their canoe and began swimming to shore. I ordered Walker to give me his rifle. I began firing at them with it, lying in a prone position, but I couldn't see where my bullets were hitting.

I asked Sergeant Tom (my tent mate), who was nearby, to spot for me, so he stood above me to help. I shot again.

"High and to the left." I adjusted my aim and fired again.

"Shoot a little more left and directly down 'bout an inch."

This time, I put a tracer round in the rifle, fired it, and watched the path of the bullet hit one of the swimmers in the head.

(Tracer rounds are bullets, coated with phosphorous, so they glow red their entire flight.)

I had another one of those short, *slow-mo* experiences as the tracer left the barrel of the rifle, and ended my *film* when the bullet entered my target's head. The person I shot hit the water and never resurfaced.

Tom slapped me on the back and said, "Powell, you're the best shot I've ever seen!"

I blushed, as I looked him square in the eyes. "Thanks to your spotting for me!" I was very proud of my marksmanship, but troubled by my cowardly deed. I had just violated my promise to God that I would only fire if lives were in jeopardy. I put that thought aside.

This concept needs to be worked on when I find time to think clearly.

That was kill number three for me.

We returned to our hill that evening. On my watch that night, I started thinking about killing people, again. I came up with an answer that would work for me while I was in 'Nam. I wasn't positive that it would work for me when I was back home, out of harm's way.

I concluded that the people I had killed, and those I may kill in the future, are enemies. They might have gone on to kill my buddies or me if I hadn't killed them.

That felt right to me. It didn't address the intoxicating adrenalin rush that hit me every time I was successful. It did let me continue to perform my duties at the highest level I was capable of achieving. Having said that to myself, I got back to the task of fighting my war.

I was still enraged at Walker for putting me in a position where I could have easily killed a fellow Marine. The next morning I headed directly to the company office. I asked to speak to the Captain, the very same one who had confronted the murderer of that VC captive I saw shot in the head.

"Sir, with all due respect, I will not serve another minute with Walker. He refused a direct order to reload my launcher, and he threatened to kill me."

"I'll take care of the situation. Return to your quarters."

Walker was on a truck headed back to the Battalion area before dusk that evening. I chose to use Private Allen instead of Walker as my A-Gunner.

Allen, who had been with another rocket team, was transferred to work with me. Allen had been in country over a month, and came highly recommended. He was a kid, too, about to turn nineteen. Sometimes, when he looked at me, I was reminded of Bambi, the deer in that old Walt Disney animation. Allen had been in country longer than me, but he didn't have good launcher firing skills. He seemed happy enough being A-Gunner. He was strong, and he was quick on his feet.

December 20th, 1966 was a particularly muggy, hot day. Walker and I weren't speaking to each other. The patrol we were on had neared the halfway point. We had one more rice paddy to cross before we reached the upper causeway. Once there, we'd take a break and turn around for home.

The rice paddy had tree lines on either end of it, and an open space to the left of its thirty-by-thirty yard area. As I looked to my left I could see a portion of the causeway.

We always crossed areas like that the same way. When "Point" reached the first tree line, we all crouched down in place and waited for our turn to advance. After "Point" ran to the far tree line, our squad advanced one position closer to the takeoff place. One by one we ran through the clearing until the whole squad had crossed.

I told Allen to be in position to cross as soon as I took off. I wasn't sure he'd obey, but I had no other alternative except to trust him. I was at the take off point. I looked back at Allen one last time, and then began running, watching only where my next step would be.

I should have been looking up, too, 'cause Jimmy (another tent mate of mine) had come to a stop halfway through the crossing. His A-Gunner had passed him by and entered the other tree line. I almost ran into Jim when all of a sudden several VC, lying prone on the causeway, ambushed us.

My *slow-mo* kicked in again. A bullet, moving at what seemed like one inch per second from my left to my right, grazed the back of Jim's flak jacket. As it inched it's was across his back, I saw it rip through the cloth. It looked like a thread was being pulled out of his jacket. I was transfixed, and stared at this amazing sight.

Of course the AK-47 has a muzzle velocity of 700 meters per second, but time seemed to almost stand still for me at that moment. I broke away from my hypnotic state. I had been shot.

I didn't feel any pain, but the force of the bullet turned me completely around. I spun to the ground and landed on my left side. I was conscious, but not really "all there." I rolled onto my back and looked at the lightly clouded sky above. At that disoriented moment I could have been almost anywhere on God's green Earth, staring skyward.

Was this it? Am I to see Heavenly Father as I ascended to Heaven? Have I descended Toward Hell, where I'd atone for my sins? Why is it so quiet? Why no pain? Ouch! There is pain! My chest is on fire. Surely, this is the gateway to Hell! Father, help me!

Another bullet whizzed over my head and I was back in 'Nam. I rolled over onto my belly and grabbed the launcher. I saw, to my dismay, that the rocket in my launcher had fallen out of the breech and onto the ground. I checked the "Arm/Disarm" switch to make sure it was in the off position, and then reloaded the launcher. I turned the switch to "Arm" and I and fired off a 'HEAT' round at the attackers.

(HEAT is an acronym for a "High Explosive Anti-Tank" rocket that penetrates targets, but doesn't contain any white phosphorus powder.)

It exploded on the causeway, kicked up some dirt, but didn't hit anybody. The VC didn't respond to my fire.

Where is everybody? Did they all get killed?

I was hot and cold simultaneously.

I HATED that launcher! My rocket rounds were labeled "Manufactured: 1955." No wonder I had had so much trouble with them.

Where was a rifle? Maybe this was Purgatory! I KNEW this would happen to me!

The *slow-mo* sensation left me.

Jimmy fled into the tree line ahead. I looked back for Allen and saw that he stood in the tree line I had just exited. I yelled at him to come and reload the launcher. That was his job, after all.

Instead of rushing to my side, Allen stayed in the tree line, knelt down on his right knee. He looked at me, sure enough, but his head shook a firm "No! No!"

Bullets continued to fly overhead. All I could do was lie as flat on the ground as possible, and pray that I wouldn't get shot again. I was scared out of my mind and disgusted that, for the second time in three months, I had been abandoned under fire.

*This is the **honor** the Corps holds dear?* echoed through my brain, bouncing around the walls of my empty skull.

Sergeant Laulu, our squad leader that day, appeared in the other tree line with Jim's machine gun team by his side. Laulu was a five-seven, two hundred pound, rock of a man. His Samoan skin was a dark golden brown, with intricate tattooing that decorated his exposed upper arms.

At that moment, I truly was in love with him.

My heart sang a tender melody to me when he and Jim's machine gun team entered the rice paddy and sprayed the causeway with heavy fire. The VCs were long gone and my life-threatening experience ended.

Now a black, murderous cloud took hold of me. I stood and turned toward the tree line and slowly, deliberately, made my way back to Allen. I intended to put a real bad hurt on him, probably sending him to the rear for emergency dental reconstruction.

When I reached his position, Allen had already retreated another three meters. He pointed his rifle directly at my chest. His jaw muscles strained to keep his bite tightly together, and his eyes, wide open, stared at me.

I knew that Allen would have killed me if I took another step toward him. The risk I faced if I kicked the rifle he held failed to change his aim he'd kill me! My world came to a standstill. In that split second, Allen and I were the only people on the planet, and he had the upper hand in our death drama.

I instantly changed my attitude; looked down at my wound, and said to him, "Tell the Corpsman I need some help here!" That ended the confrontation, thankfully. I was filled to the brim with a fear of confrontation. That fear would plague me for years and years.

I examined myself thoroughly. My flak jacket had absorbed most of the impact, and left me with a superficial cut across the left side of my rib-cage. Ironically, the Corpsman who treated my wound was the same one who had attended to the woman I'd killed some time ago.

I learned more lessons that day. Everywhere was dangerous. There were no safe places. Every one around me was dangerous. I vowed to *never again* confront people.

Months later I found out that the Corpsman hadn't put me in for a Purple Heart. I guessed it was payback for killing the woman, or something like that.

Although Allen threatened to kill me, I chose to put his actions aside and mentally excused him for his cowardice. From then on, I kept one "eye" on Allen at all times in case he reacted toward me the same way he had again. I was constantly troubled about that, but the tension I felt diminished over time. We worked well in the field together and my memories of Allen's threat to me gradually receded into the back of my mind.

After the rocket launcher ammunition failed me, yet again, I decided that my team would carry M72 LAAWs (Light Anti-Armor Weapon) on all patrols, and carry the launcher only when we were on operations. The LAAW was a shoulder-fired, 66-millimeter rocket, similar in effect to a 3.5-inch rocket, except that the launcher was made of Fiberglass, and was disposable after one shot. That way, I could carry a rifle and have more firepower available to the patrol.

I carried four LAAWs, crisscrossed behind my back, and my A-Gunner did the same. Instead of four rockets, we now had eight. We also added another rifleman to the patrol: me.

4 The Sixth Commandment

In January the Vietnamese celebrate TET. I seem to remember it's like our New Year's Day. We went out on another operation that day, except we were ordered to hold our fire, even if we were attacked. If we were attacked, the command would decide if, and when, we were to retaliate. We were out two days. We captured an Asian man, who looked like a very fit, very large non-Vietnamese person to me. He escaped our control within an hour after being taken. I suspect that he was released, rather than a clever escapee.

When we returned to our hill, I thought *we were never attacked, and we never initiated an attack of our own. Two full days of peace! Why don't they make this holiday of theirs last a lifetime?* Alas, this was not to be. We continued being killed, and killing.

All in all, I know that I killed at least five Vietnamese people. I know this because each one was with my rifle and there was no way of forgetting. I saw each of my victims through the sights of my rifle when I shot them, and saw them fall when I hit them.

I believed that we should obey the Ten Commandments. I didn't do that, and it was/is not easy to live with that knowledge.

Thou shall not kill.

I knew I had broken that Commandment, and I was burdened with remorse before the time I had taken the life of my fifth victim.

I justified my actions to myself while I was in 'Nam. In order to stay alive and return home from this war, in one piece, hopefully, I vowed a few simple things of myself. I will "do my duty to the best of my ability," protect my life, limbs, sight, and hearing, protect my comrades, treat non-hostile citizens with a modicum of respect, stay clean of disease, stay sober and alert, and acquire the respect I thought I would receive as a patriot who served his country with honor and in good faith.

Then the following thought hit me, **and hit me hard**:

I was wounded. I wounded and killed people to save my mortal life, but I have forgotten about my immortal life.

I sought out Biblical passages that might help me come to grips with my guilt. I had a pocket-sized Bible with me that I kept underneath my cot. I found a particular scripture that I read, and reread often. It's from the Book of Luke. I copied it onto a piece of paper that I carried in the right rear pocket of my trousers. It read:

"And he turned to the woman, and said unto Simon, Seest thou this woman? I entered into thine house, thou gavest me no water for my feet: but she hath washed my feet with tears, and wiped them with the hairs of her head. Thou gavest me no kiss: but this woman since the time I came in hath not ceased to kiss my feet. My head with oil thou didst not anoint: but this woman hath anointed my feet with ointment. Wherefore I say unto thee, Her sins, which are many, are forgiven; for she loved much: but to whom little is forgiven, the same loveth little. And he said unto her, Thy sins are forgiven. And they that sat at meat with him began to say within themselves, Who is this that forgiveth sins also? And he said to the woman, Thy faith hath saved thee; go in peace."

That meant a lot to me, "thy faith hath saved thee," but it didn't tell me how to demonstrate my faith sufficiently to be saved on Judgment Day.

My decision to show my faith took the form of ritualistic prayer. I have said The Lord's Prayer every day since mid-May 1967.

•   •   •

I went on another day patrol... The patrol area was a familiar one. I nonchalantly walked along, and daydreamed of going home.

Because it was familiar terrain, I felt safe in the location, a *big mistake* to make any time in 'Nam. From the tree line about thirty meters to my left, shots whizzed in and cracked the air before I heard the now unpleasantly-familiar rifle "pops." I instinctively hit the deck, and my comrades

Suiting up for another patrol (1/27/1967). Source: DWP

did the same. We returned fire I lay prone on the ground, and aimed at the direction I thought the enemy fire came from. The outline of a little child, four to six years old, caught my attention. *Too bad*, I said to myself, *that's the wrong place to be, little one!*

I hollered "Cease Fire" to the left of me, then turned to my right and said the same thing. The rifleman on my left took aim, fired, and hit the child.

I looked at him with disgust and shock. He looked back and said "Don't say anything to anyone about that!"

I didn't, and I wouldn't. I learned earlier on, with my "Allen" experience, that confrontation with men who commit bad acts was very, very dangerous.

I watched in amazement as an old man, who cried and shook, dressed in a tan pajama outfit, face shriveled up like a prune, picked up and carried the child, a girl, straight out of the tree line and toward our positions. Strangely, I felt no compassion for the kid.

Our Corpsman attended to the child's wound. He patched up her left leg. Fortunately, it was a superficial wound to her thigh.

She wore a light blue dress: too cute to forget.

Have I become that depraved, to simply look the other way when a young child is attacked?

YES, I had!

• • •

The operations we went on placed us in great jeopardy. When we were home on our hill, the daily patrols left us time to *act* normal.

"Mail Call" was a daily ritual. While one man called out the names on the packages and envelopes, another man accepted our outbound letters. I wrote to my wife and parents every day I could. My letters home kept my incoming mail flow pretty constant.

After every patrol, I cleaned my rifle, the magazines that held my bullets, and even the bullets themselves. Afterward, I waited for the mail to come, read it, ate C-rations, drank Kool-Aid or hot chocolate, read Bible passages, and wrote back home.

After I wrote my letters, I talked with the other men in the tent about this-and-that, but never about our 'Nam experiences.

More than one letter from my wife, Kathy, deeply upset me. She was honest to a fault, even when it could hurt her then, or in the future. She told me that she was doing fine, and missed me terribly, and all that kind of stuff. Sometimes she went on to say that she and some girlfriends enjoyed going out nights to drink and dance. She described these outings in more detail than I cared to learn. That was the *honest to a fault* part I mentioned.

It felt like she had written me "goodbye" letters, and I was crushed! I wrote her back each time and told her that I didn't want to know how much fun she was having while I was out fighting to save my life. She kept it up, though. I held that against her, strongly against her.

Some men smoked marijuana to kill the time and numb the psychological pain. They called them "Thai Sticks." Apparently they were laced with some other narcotic and were stronger than the usual pot.[6] Others preferred to drink copious amounts of beer. Almost every one tried to numb their mind to what was going on, trying anything to cope with their anger, fear, guilt, hate, and loneliness.

I did none of those things. "Death" could come knock at my door any minute, I believed, and I wanted to be perfectly prepared for the fight.

•   •   •

Occasionally, when the "Command" decided to improve the reinforcement of our hill, we took a truck back to Battalion for supplies. That was a twenty-minute ride each way, over bumps, down dips, and around narrow turns.

Usually, we would either pick up barbed wire or empty sandbags. If it were a "wire run," we would promptly turn around and take the load back to the hill. If we were given sandbags, we would load up the bags and shovels and head to the coast of the Red Sea, a half-hour ride to the beach and a half-hour ride back to Battalion, and fill them with sand.

I made a sandbag run shortly after I joined Delta. I was still under the impression that I was there to protect the South Vietnamese people.

When the truck stopped and we started filling the bags with sand, a group of Vietnamese boys and girls came up to our truck. There were six or seven of them, ranging in age from four to twelve. They all wore T-shirts of various colors, and the usual pajama trousers, also differently colored. A twelve-year-old girl stood out.

She had a sweet smile and spoke some English.

"GIs Number One; VC Number Ten," she chanted a couple of times.

That meant GIs Number One, (the best), VC Number Ten (the worst).

---

[6] There are rumors that 'Thai Stick' has been used to describe Cannabis laced with Opium or Hashish oil, but we know of no data to support this. (Source: www.erowid.org)

Girl at sandbag site (01/17/1967). Source: DWP

"You have candy, GI?"

I had some C-ration chocolate bars and gave them to her. She shared them with the other kids. We finished our sandbag business and returned to the hill without incident.

Nearly seven months passed before I returned to gather more sand. Having been on many, many patrols during that interlude, I learned that everything, and everybody, was dangerous.

The Vietnamese, in my opinion, all hated our presence in their country. Ironically, the same little girl was at the sand dune where we were taking sand. She, and a few friends, approached the truck.

I was standing guard at the time and when she refused my commands to "Dee, Dee" (Vietnamese, for "Go, Go") I smashed her head with the butt of my rifle. She grabbed her cheek with her left hand as she fell to the ground. There was some minor swelling, but her skin was unbroken.

I had heard that the VC used children as weapons. The child would detonate hand grenades, dynamite, or other explosive devices when they were near U. S. troops. I suspected the girl was one of them when she refused to go away.

I felt like a cruel child abuser after I struck her, but my flawed thoughts insisted I protect myself and my men from this potential danger. She looked up at me with a stunned, questioning glance. I looked away and wallowed in my remorse for hurting an innocent kid.

I've become a beast of a man! I am no better than the men I loathed when I first got here!

On watch that night, I reflected on the events of that day. I recognized that my spiritual and emotional being was not that of the man I was before all the combat I had endured. I pitied myself, but made no promises to myself that I would change my future behavior.

5 These are My Demons

"This war is a bitch for the front-line infantryman[7]."
— David B. Schulberg interviewed by William Tuohy

At the base of our hill stood a small Ville. Thirty-some villagers lived there. We would occasionally go down to the little village to buy stuff and loaf around. There, we could buy candles and a few other goodies to make tent life more bearable. There was a family that laundered our dirty fatigues and then returned them dry and folded for a few cents.

I had returned from an intense, dangerous patrol earlier that morning and was wound up pretty tight. Unfortunately, I decided to pick up my

Ville at the base of Hill 41 (02/07/1967). Source: DWP

---

[7] "Soldier Sees '2 Different Wars' in Vietnam Stint", *LA Times*, Nov. 29th, 1967, pg. 17.

laundry that day. I checked the bundle the man handed me and found that several of my trousers were missing. I demanded that he find and return them to me right away.

"No, GI. No more clothes. Get out!"

I stepped back about a meter and pointed my rifle at his chest.

"I'll kill you if you don't give me my pants right now!"

The laundryman's luck was with him that day. An officer immediately intervened and ordered me to return to the hill. The officer saved that man's life.

I'm mere seconds away from killing a man over a pair of pants! I'm unraveling fast.

It was blatantly obvious to me that my anger threshold was unacceptably low. Rage lay in wait in my psyche just a "click" below being angry or upset.

That scared me. Worse, I carried that hyper-vigilant attitude home from 'Nam and with me for decades to follow.

• • •

Artillery flares have a little parachute attached to them, inside the WP canister. When the canister reaches its maximum height, it explodes and ejects the flare, and then the parachute opens. The empty canister falls to the ground as the flare floats down slowly.

One night on a large operation, I was trying to rest before my watch came up. I heard what sounded like a small toy airplane flying above me. The overhead noise got louder and louder. I put my helmet back on and pulled it tightly onto my skull. I crouched like a baseball catcher and wondered what would happen next. An object smashed into the muddy ground just inches from my face. It turned out to be an exploded, empty canister from a flare round.

Had it hit me, I would have probably died. Now, even the sky above was dangerous!

• • •

On another company-sized operation, I took a short break from the march, and rested on the side of a hill, bathed in warm sunlight. It was not unusual to have insects of all sorts irritate me. When I heard a swarm of bees around my head, I was surprised, because I hadn't noticed bees, bee-hives, honey, or other things I associated with that insect in Vietnam.

My attention was drawn to little puffs of dirt being kicked up on the ground near where I sat. All of a sudden it dawned on me: those were bullets "humming" around my head, and they kicked up dirt right next to me. They came from far enough away that I didn't hear the familiar "pop" from the rifle barrels. I scrambled for cover in an instant.

• • •

If a serviceman had two Purple Hearts, each of which required at least 48 hours of hospitalization, then he was kept away from combat after the second hospital stay. If a man received three Purple Hearts, he was immediately taken out of harm's way. In some ways, then, there was a reason to incur "enemy" wounds.

Some men took drastic measures to get out of 'Nam. One way was to fake an injury from a booby trap. One or more men collaborated to throw a hand grenade into the brush near them; close enough to cause fragmentary wounds to them, yet far enough away to avoid serious consequences. That act was called "Fragging".

Their goal was to get Purple Hearts so they could get pulled out.

I saw two riflemen Frag themselves. Garcia, who was a guitar-playing Mexican-American, and another runt of a man I didn't know, were on patrol with me one murky afternoon. Garcia asked me if I wanted "in" on the scheme. I said "absolutely not" and backed away from him quickly.

The two of them stood shoulder-to-shoulder, facing away from the brush. The runt pulled the pin and threw the grenade about two meters away from them, then both of them quickly covered their groins with their folded hands.

It exploded; they were hit with some shrapnel. Both of them were treated by a Corpsman, and Garcia was Medevac'ed. He was hit, among other places, in the left hand and lost his ring finger in the process. That ended his guitar career forever. They both were awarded a Purple Heart medal.

Later on, a small Italian kid named Tony-something, shot himself in the foot during a firefight we were involved in, severing one of his toes. He was Medevac'ed. A few weeks later, he was back in his former squad. I went on a night ambush with his squad a night or two after he rejoined his unit. I heard him crying as he slept before his watch came up. He got a Purple Heart, too.

• • •

VC committed suicide in a tunnel rather than facing capture.
Source: DWP

I was on another operation when we stopped and set up a perimeter around the command group. I heard a dull explosion to the rear of my position, near where the Officers gathered. There was some hollering and scuffling, then silence.

Within minutes two men walked from the area where the noises had originated. They carried a large, round, flat basket. On it was the body of a VC whose hands and face were blown off.

He had been hiding in a tunnel with a trap door and was discovered there by an alert grunt. Rather than surrender and leave his tunnel, he exploded a hand grenade that he clutched to his face.

The men laid the body about ten meters in front of my position and left it there for me to stare at for over an hour. The smell was haunting. I thought that I smelled a lamb, roasting in an oven. The scent haunts me today. It seemed to have come through my nose, then curled up the back of my skull, over the top of my brain, then descended into my nose again.

I will never forget that sensation.

I could taste him.

•   •   •

As I stood watch one day, our supply truck approached the hill. I watched it come up the road and saw the truck get ambushed. They didn't stop and fight, but continued at full speed up the road and into our perimeter.

I ran to the side of the truck to see what happened, and what I could do to help the men. The truck bed was filled with barbed wire that we used to protect our perimeter.

One man rode in the back with the wire bundles. He had been shot in his head during the ambush. As I looked at his face, I saw him die before my very eyes. I knew him only by his nickname, "Bear."

The driver said one of the attackers was wearing a blue sweater. I turned to look where the attack occurred and observed a Vietnamese man, in a blue sweater, walking with two other men in the opposite direction, away from our hill.

I snapped! My mind had broken. I'd lost all sense of self-protection.

In a garbled voice, I yelled "Come on!" to whoever would listen, then headed straight down the road after the man in blue. I had thrown my personal safety to the wind and marched out in the open. I wanted to kill any living thing I could see, be it insect, bird, animal, or human. Other men shouted at me to take cover in the tree lines.

I gradually regained my sanity. Though it was brief in actual time, it had seemed *forever* that I had been crazy and reckless.

A couple of our men, including the Gunny (Gunnery Sergeant) from the company office, captured the "sweater man" and another with him. I returned to the hill and went to the mess hall to get some lunch. The captives were led to a spot right next to the mess hall, then blindfolded and told to squat down.

A Viet Cong prisoner awaits interrogation at the A-109 Special Forces Detachment in Thuong Duc (25km west of Da Nang) 01/23/1967. Source: National Archives.

They squatted in plain sight of me. I distracted myself by eating some chili and beans. I told Mack, another of my tent mates sitting across the table from me, that the one in blue probably killed "Bear."

"So, what the heck can you do about it?" he said.

"Watch this!" I laid my spoon atop my unfinished beans, walked out of the mess hall, over to the crouched man in blue, and gave him one of my best Karate side kicks across the bridge of his nose.

He flew back a good three meters, landed on his butt, and bled profusely. His crying brought a Corpsman to his aid.

I came back in to finish lunch and said, "**That's** what I can do about it!"

Mack complimented me on my kicking style. We finished eating and parted company. Later on, the captives were taken away in a Huey (helicopter) for imprisonment.

Inside, I felt as though, in some small way, I had avenged "Bear." I always **hated** the orders we had to obey when it came to fighting this war. We were forbidden to shoot first, even when there was a clear reason that danger was impending.

My internal dialog screamed out in my mind: I detested the Vietnamese. I detested the war. I detested the intense feelings of rage, fear, anger, embarrassment, disgust, repulsion, revulsion, shame, and my inferiority complex that had been greatly intensified in my mind.

The kick I gave my enemy that afternoon somehow made me feel redeemed, self-righteous and proud. Sane people may not comprehend that idea.

When we were not on patrol we were given chores to do. One of the tasks we were assigned to do was to strategically string bundles of barbed wire around the perimeter.

I was on a working party laying wire on one of those days. It was a sunny afternoon. One of the bundles I picked up to move had human brain tissue embedded into its coils.

I immediately flashed back to the moment when "Bear" had died before my eyes in the ambushed truck.

I was there!

In slow motion, I moved through my memory, step by step. I watched "Bear" die again. When my "film" ended, I wept.

•   •   •

The Corps never told us what was in store for us. In April 1967, they told us that the Army's 196th Light Infantry Brigade was going to take over our lines and we were going up North. How far up they didn't say.

Am I going to Da Nang, or the DMZ? Where am I going to now?

"What do we do with the Army personnel when they get on the hill?" I asked.

"Train them about working in the field here."

The Army men were with us for about a week. We packed up all our gear in our Sea Bags and made room for the new guys to settle into our tents. We took them on our regular patrols so they knew a little about the area they would protect after we left.

On patrol, spread out to avoid being an easy sniper target. Source: DWP

That was harrowing, to say least. Marines knew to stay spread out on patrol, leaving ten or more meters between each other. The Army personnel did not have that discipline. They bunched up in twos and threes as they wandered along with us. I was extremely uncomfortable with this behavior. I knew that they would draw attention to our presence in the field, and thus they would become choice targets for snipers.

On one hand, I was grateful that we finally shipped out, just to be far, far away from the sloppy Army fieldwork. On the other hand, I was fearful and clueless about where we were going. It was far enough away that we were flown to our destination in cargo planes, after helicopters took us to the Chu Lai airbase.

Our new Tactical Area of Responsibility was 20 miles southwest of Da Nang airbase, specifically Hill 55 (a.k.a. "Camp Muir"), deep in the countryside, again. It was located in the Rocket Belt area. That's where the NVA launched their rocket attacks at the Da Nang airbase.

There was no "takeover" for us, unlike the one we gave the Army unit who took over our Chu Lai address. We began patrolling the area as if we had been there for years. It was as tough and dangerous as our old place, but we learned how to work the area as safely as possible and still get our job done; protect and save the South Vietnamese people.

Hill 55 was large enough to hold all four companies in the Battalion. This meant that not everyone knew what the next unit was doing. This lack of communication almost got my whole patrol wiped out one day.

I was returning to the hill from the field (the Tic Phu's, 5.5km southwest of the hill) I think, near the river and the bridge that spanned it. As I got to the last tree line before the barbed wire, I heard the sound of fighter planes approaching.

The patrol came to a stop and I watched the aircraft head straight for our position. The F-4 Phantoms were ours, of course. The Viet Cong had no aerial capabilities. To our bewilderment they began firing their 20mm M61 cannons at us, with an effective rate of more than 100 rounds per second. Any one of those rounds could have ended my life right there.

To a man, we dived to the ground and scrambled for deep cover. I looked up as one of the fighters passed over us, about fifty meters above ground. He dropped a fragmentation bomb in front of our position and I watched it fall from the belly of the plane, arm itself, and detonate.

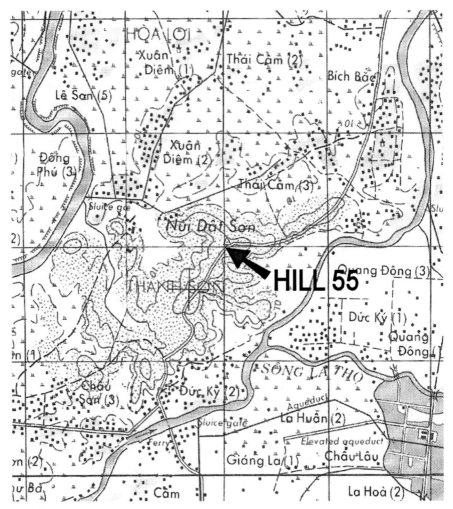

Hill 55 TAOR. Map courtesy USGS (Map 6640-IV, coords AT 970620)
Scale: each box is 1km square

There were a few more bomb runs, and some more strafing, and then they flew away. Apparently, someone on the hill had mistaken our patrol for one of the enemy's. Again, I wanted desperately to go home. The sky was truly dangerous, all right.

•   •   •

M16 Assault Rifle

I could go on and on about the M16 rifle. I got my M16 about six months into my tour. They replaced the M14 rifle I knew well, and trusted. The M16 frequently jammed, making it inoperable. We complained bitterly. To resolve the problem, we were given orders that our M16's *did* work, that they *did* not jam.

The rifle didn't get any better, but the complaints about them were outlawed. The first M16 rifles issued to US troops in Vietnam severely jammed in combat, resulting in numerous casualties.

First off, the US Army replaced the originally specified Dupont IMR powder with standard ball powder, as used in 7.62x51mm NATO ammunition. The ball powder produced much more fouling, which quickly jammed the actions of the M16 unless the gun was cleaned well and often.

This, pitifully combined with the fact that the initial M16 rifles were promoted by the Colt as "low maintenance." So, for the sake of economy, no cleaning supplies were procured for new M16 rifles, and no weapon care training was conducted for the troops. As a result, soldiers did not know how to clean their rifles, and had no provisions for cleaning, and things soon turned bad.

To add to the trouble, the ball powder also had a different pressure curve, so they produced higher pressures at the gas port, giving rise to the rate of fire, and, thus, decreasing accuracy and increasing parts wear.

The first magazines only held twenty rounds compared to the Soviet AK-47, which had a thirty round capacity. Bugs were worked out, but not until well after my tour.[8]

---

[8] Source: Modern Firearms & Ammunition (http://world.guns.ru/)

I resolved to know my new weapon intimately. I disassembled it much like a surgeon performs an autopsy. The chamber, where the bullet entered the rifle barrel, was notched. The bolt was notched to correspond to the chamber. There was no room for error. If a speck of dirt, or sand, or whatever interfered with the locking of the bolt to the chamber, the rifle was rendered useless.

We had no transitional training from the M14 to the M16. We were expected to use the new, "improved" rifle like we were changing from one pair of socks to the next. The Marines who assaulted Hill 880 (I think that was the hill) found out that the new rifle was a nightmare. Many men died trying to get their weapon to work in the midst of their battle.

I cleaned my new piece meticulously. I used "Q-Tips" to clean the notches. I rammed facial swabs up and down the barrel. I oiled each round, in each of my four magazines, and stretched the springs of each one, until I believed they would push up the next round flawlessly. Still, I had a horrible feeling that it would fail me in the heat of battle.

Prestridge on patrol. Source: DWP.

Shortly after we were given our "improved" weapons, I was on patrol with a mate named Prestridge. He was, at that time, the youngest man to be engaged in combat. He could not have been a day over 18 years old. He was a big kid, handsome and tall, and very self-confident.

Prestridge had no respect for the Vietnamese. To see how well his new rifle would work, he shot a woman as she gathered a bucket of water from a well.

"Just test-firing the thing, Powell."

• • •

Once, and only once, we took some "ARVN" (Army of the Republic of South Viet Nam) soldiers with us on a platoon-sized patrol. An ARVN, who walked next to me, began horsing around with his .30 caliber rifle. He fired short bursts into the air.

That alarmed some VC in the hills near us. They opened fire on the column. I saw where their fire originated and I shot off a WP round at them. When it exploded, some of the powder landed on a water buffalo cow that was grazing nearby. The cow went straight up in the air about three feet, came down, and then ran like a thoroughbred racehorse.

I laughed out loud. That was an extremely amusing sight!

Unlike the North Vietnamese Army, the ARVN was not known for its professionalism. PFC David B. Schulberg quipped:

> "It's a loused-up war. I wouldn't mind it so much if the ARVNs would fight harder. But most of the time they don't do a thing—no leadership, sitting around in their base camps drinking beer. If they want their freedom they should fight harder for it than they've been doing."[9]

• • •

---

[9] "Soldier Sees '2 Different Wars' in Vietnam Stint", *LA Times*, Nov. 29th, 1967. p. 17.

I had my share of minuscule aches and pains. I awoke in the morning a few days into an operation, when I had to sleep under my poncho one rainy night, to find a buffalo leech on my left chinbone. It was four inches long and two inches in circumference. I put the lit end of my cigarette on its back to make it fall off.

The leech was engorged with my blood. I put it in a C-ration stove with a heat tab, lit the tab and burned it for five minutes. Another leech was so full of my blood, it fell off my leg without being coaxed. I roasted it, too.

I had a half-dollar sized spot of jungle rot on my right forearm that refused to heal. I bear the scars of the leech and the jungle rot to this day.

On a daylight patrol, near a river whose name I never knew, I passed out. My buddies helped me to 'D' Medical Quarters, where I was hooked up to an intravenous feeding tube for forty eight hours, dripping sugar water into my vein.

I had gastrointestinal parasites, the result of drinking untreated water I had consumed from wells in the Villes I had patrolled.

Back home, I had a relapse of stomach problems weeks after being released from active duty. My wife, Kathy came home from work and found me writhing on the floor of our living room, lying in a fetal position with both forearms crossed and squeezing my abdomen tightly.

A Doctor visit and a sigmoidectomy revealed a small colony of hookworms nestled near the beginning of my large intestine. Four days of drinking a foul medicine took care of that problem.

6 R&R Honolulu and a Look Back

A nother one of the cruelties of the Vietnam War was that they gave us Rest and Recuperation (R&R). That meant that after I had served in country for a certain amount of time, usually three or four months, I could leave Vietnam and take a "mini-vacation".

I could leave my personal war for from five to seven days. The seven-day R&R locations were Sydney, Australia and Honolulu, Hawaii.

I had been in combat for seven months. By then, I knew that I was not going to survive my war. I decided to go see my wife one last time.

I chose Honolulu for my R&R port. Kathy (my wife of two years) and I were both familiar with the island of Oahu, where Honolulu is located. She was born there. I went to the University of Hawaii after high school graduation, as a reward for being a good student. My folks paid my way 'cause I'd earned good grades.

Finally getting to go on R&R was wonderful, but it turned out to be quite difficult. I received my R&R dates for April 1967. I wrote Kathy and told her to make arrangements for us in Honolulu, and book herself on a round trip airplane flight. She wrote back that she had done so, and had paid for the trip.

The day before I was scheduled to leave, another Marine unit, stationed down the coast to the south of our position, captured what was then the largest cache (storage) of enemy weapons and munitions since the war began.

The Marines needed reinforcement right away; three Battalions of North Vietnamese Army (NVA) soldiers had surrounded them. The cache was located just inland from the sea. My company was ordered to reinforce the trapped, gravely endangered Marines.

I told the First Sergeant that I was scheduled to leave the next day for R&R. He told me that nothing was more important than the lives of fellow Marines and that I was going along, like it or not.

I agreed with that. I disagreed with his decision to order me to go with all the others.

Will my being there assure the success of the rescue?

A rhetorical question: I knew it wouldn't, but I had to follow orders.

We boarded helicopters and flew out to the battle. Naturally, we came under heavy fire when we landed and rushed out of the choppers.

As I was running out of the rear of my chopper, I struck my head on the exit doorway, and I fell face down in the sand at the bottom of the ramp. The rest of the men exited the chopper and ran into the woods. No one made an attempt to help me to my feet.

I managed to get up by myself and joined them in the tree line.

In my mind's eye, I had been abandoned under fire for the third time.

We established our perimeter lines and all stayed awake all night. There were no attacks then, or the next morning. I was confused about that until I realized that the skies were filled with our planes, and a Navy Destroyer was just offshore.

We were ordered to march back to our company lines, walking along the shoreline for about ten miles. The Destroyer sailed alongside our marching column the entire distance. The NVA followed us all the way back to our area, but never made contact.

When we reached our hill I found out that I could still make my R&R departure if I hurried. I ran to my tent in a panic, took off my fatigues and boots, and flung them on my cot. I opened my Sea bag and took out my Marine Corps Tropical uniform, put the pants on, put my shoes on and tied them, zipped up my trousers, and put on my shirt.

I ran to the almost-departed supply truck headed back to Battalion headquarters. I buttoned up my shirt as I ran. Another Marine from Bravo Company, PFC Warnecki, was headed for the same R&R destination and was already on the truck when I jumped aboard.

Warnecki was a friendly guy from Atlanta, Georgia. He said he had a Polish bloodline and his parents moved from Poland to Georgia when he was still a babe in his momma's arms. What skin of his wasn't tan was porcelain white. I teased him about that as we got to know a little about each other on the way to Chu Lai.

We were both skinny and tired, but there was nothing we could do about that. We were also unarmed, so we lay prone in the back of the series of trucks that transported us from Battalion, to Regimental headquarters, to Division headquarters, and then to the Chu Lai airstrip.

We boarded another Continental Airlines 707 that had just dropped its load of fresh troops from Okinawa. We flew to Okinawa. However, before we could depart, the plane refueled while we sat in the cabin. The pilot announced that we could get off and stretch if we wanted, but Warnecki and I didn't budge.

During the long flight to Honolulu, I thought about how my life had developed before any of this Vietnam business started. I knew what kind of person I had become, an uncaring, emotional man who was consumed with guilt and remorse. I needed to remember the "David" I had been.

I reflected on my past, as best I could. I recited to myself the following: I was born in Los Angeles, California in 1941. I was healthy, weighed seven pounds, eight ounces and measured twenty-two inches in length: an average newborn by all physical measures.

My mom, dad, and I lived in a small duplex in East Los Angeles until I turned four years old. World War II started right after I was born. The war ended in '45, and my parents and I moved to Long Beach, California. We lived there until I was seven. We lived close to Belmont Shores (a small bay). Mom took me to the bay for swimming lessons and playtime. I loved those days and learned to swim before I turned five.

I had fun in school, but was a very timid child. When I was seven, we moved into my grandfather's house in Pasadena, California.

Mom and I moved without dad. Dad was having an extra-marital affair. When mom found this out, she told grandpa. We moved in with him, without dad. She later forgave him and he moved in with us.

When I was nine years old, mom and dad had Susan, my little sister.

My parents made it very clear to me that I should develop a strong work ethic. I became an after-school newspaper delivery boy at ten years of age. I kept the route until I was fourteen. My grades began to slip, so I gave up the paper route and concentrated on my homework.

In junior high school, my height stalled at five-foot four, and I was miserable. I had a growth spurt of four inches in one summer and then continued to grow more gradually, to my present height of six feet.

When I was sixteen, we had an in-ground swimming pool installed. I became the unofficial pool maintenance man, or "pool boy." I took full advantage of our pool and its diving board.

After I got my driver's license I was able to go on a few dates, but nothing romantic ever developed for me.

I was given a challenge by mom at the start of my senior year. If I could make all "A's and B's", I would "win" a summer vacation by myself in Hawaii. I did.

I had a wonderful summer. I enrolled at the University of Hawaii. I dropped the class after the first week. I swam every day in the waters of Waikiki and took up surfboard riding. After the third week, my conscience got the better of me and I told my folks that I had dropped out of school. They wrote and said that since the vacation was already paid for I could go ahead and enjoy my time there. "There's no hard feelings," they wrote.

I entered Pasadena City College, a two-year school in town. I enrolled, but soon dropped out. My dad worked as a data processor in Los Angeles. Dad got me a starting job, swing shift, at the same company. After six months I found a fulltime day job as a tabulating machine operator for the Southern California Edison Company. I got married and then found out I would be drafted, so I enlisted in the Corps.

HELLO! The plane is landing! You're not on watch. You're back in the world!

When my mind returned to the present, I was on the final approach to landing on Oahu.

I landed in the dead of night. In those days, in Hawaii, the airplanes loaded and unloaded their passengers by way of stairways rolled up to the side of the airplane. I had about fifty meters to walk before I entered the terminal. I chose to run.

Kathy visiting me during boot camp graduation. Source: DWP

Warnecki and I had parted company at the terminal doorway without saying another word to one another.

Inside the terminal I sort of panicked. I was in a strange place, surrounded by strangers. They were to close to me, and that frightened me. My instincts were developed to a point where being in a group was dangerous. I felt threatened. I looked around the terminal for Kathy, but didn't see her.

Kathy was a cute girl. She was five-two, a little over a hundred pounds, shapely, brown-eyed, with a warm smile.

She was there, but I didn't pick her out of the crowd. She came up and touched me on my left shoulder as I looked in the opposite direction. Suddenly, I was in the "open" and re-experienced being ambushed and wounded.

I dived to the ground and rolled over, ending up in a prone firing position. I was back in a rice paddy, wounded and helpless.

Kathy screamed! Onlookers screamed! I came to my senses, realized that I wasn't in 'Nam being attacked, and humbly rose to my feet. I didn't know it then, but I had had my first physical *and* mental flashback.

I went over and hugged Kathy tightly, and gave her a short kiss on her cheek.

"I'm so, so sorry, honey!"

We left the terminal and got in the car Kathy had rented for us. She offered me the keys, but I didn't think I could remember how to drive. She took us to the hotel room where we would stay for the next five nights.

After so much exposure to terror and trauma, I lacked any form of love, for anything. That included my wife. I thought if we made "love" that I would regain healthy emotional feelings. I tried seduction, but it felt (inside) like I raped her.

I changed out of my uniform and into the blue Levis and Hawaiian shirt Kathy brought for me to wear. We had a drink in the hotel lounge after that, and went to dinner. Before I slept, I took her again. It felt exactly like our earlier sex.

Downtown Honolulu in 1967

I did "that" every day of my "vacation." I told her that I knew I be-haved like a criminal, but it was only because I missed her so. She said she understood.

"That's all right! I love you, too!"

I drank lots of hard liquor the whole time I was on R&R. I staggered around everywhere we went. I didn't have a healthy mind, so we drove around the island much of the time, in silence. We played the tourist rou-tine, and took in all the best places to visit on Oahu.

Kathy quit asking what it was like for me in 'Nam after the first or second day. All the while I was with her, I told her that "I was absolutely unaffected by Viet Nam." I said it was "A walk in the park." Reassuringly, I said, "I'm five years older than you, and you don't need to worry about me. I'll be fine after my tour is up."

I told Kathy that I'd seen lots of ugly things that she didn't ever need to know about, but that I was going to get through it OK, and after I got back to home, back to work, and made decent money again, I'd return to normal.

I could tell she knew I lied through my teeth, but she never dared to say anything to contradict me.

On the last day, she drove me back to the airport, kissed me quickly, waited until I closed the car door, then drove off without a wave of her hand, or a look back to see if I watched her go.

I boarded my return flight to Vietnam, certain of my fate: I would be killed. I knew that if I sat on the plane and did nothing, I would work myself up into a full-blown panic. I strained to think of what I could do. Then it hit me.

I didn't want to be remembered as a foolish, "shoot-from-the-hip" jerk who had decided, one day, on a whim, to join the Marines. I chose to write a letter to my aunt and uncle explaining what led up to my enlistment. They lived in Michigan and we hadn't seen each other in years, but I knew they'd be invited to the funeral, and I knew they would appreciate knowing their nephew hadn't acted recklessly. I wrote...

_____

Dear Maryanne and Vincent,

I want you to know the circumstances that led up to my decision to enlist in the Armed Forces. I'm telling you this in the hope that, if asked, you would explain my actions to my loved ones and friends.

After reading this, you both will know the events that led up to that fateful day. No one else has fully understood my actions.

This all started in early January 1966. I arrived home from work as usual. The mail had come through the front door. I stepped over it on my way into the kitchen for a drink. I drank Scotch. I poured a tumbler-full, over ice, and sat it down on the sink. I went into the bedroom, threw my coat on the bed and loosened my tie.

I went back in the kitchen, picked up my drink and went to sort through the mail that was scattered on the rug.

"Just the usual bills," I said to myself, while I looked over the envelopes on my way over to the couch. I flopped down and finished leafing through the letters, and then it happened!

I got one of those dreaded post cards from Uncle Sam, telling me I had to go for a physical to see if I was draft material.

Why did they want to draft me? I was twenty-four years old, married, had a good job, and everything was great.

I sat there on the couch pinching the sides of the card with my fingers as hard as I could.

Maybe if I squeeze hard enough it'll disappear!

I pushed the card in my back pocket and drained my glass without a pause. *I'll call them tomorrow. This is some kind of cruel joke!*

I poured another drink and waited for Kathy to come home. After I'd had several more drinks and done a lot of pacing up and down the hall, I heard her car enter the driveway.

I gave her a kiss hello and she went into the bathroom. A short while later, she came out to where I was sitting. She knew I was upset about something.

"What's wrong?"

I didn't want to tell her. I blamed my grouchy mood on work. I made us both a drink and turned on the TV. We didn't talk much after that. We went to bed about eleven.

The next morning, after settling into my desk at work, I called the number on the card.

"Do I have to come in for this physical? I'm twenty-four and I'm married. Aren't I exempt from the draft?"

"Not unless you have kids or you're taking care of an invalid relative," the person on the other end of the line muttered in a practiced monotone. "Are you either of those things?"

"No."

"Then we'll see you on the date printed on the card. Bye, Bye!"

My stomach tightened and I had a sour taste in my mouth.

I don't have any kids. I'm screwed! What am I going to do? Can I flunk the physical? NO! What's going to happen to my career? I'm a computer programmer, in hot demand by a couple of headhunters.

It seemed like everything in my world was tumbling down. When the big day for my physical came, just before Valentine's Day, I made some lame excuse about getting my car tuned up so I could leave work. I drove over to the Induction Center in downtown L.A. around two o'clock in the afternoon.

I was supposed to report to a room on the fifth floor. The building was a typical government building, drab gray cement block construction, metal framed windows, no curtains, and older than most of the nearby business buildings.

I parked close by, walked in the building, rode the antiquated elevator to the fifth floor, got off, and handed the clerk at the admissions desk my postcard.

"Here's a locker key. Go through that door, take off all your clothes except your tee shirt and underpants, put the rest of your stuff in the locker and take the key with you while you're inside." What a little wimp he was. He was an eighteen year old, skinny nerd. He had a squeaky, girly voice.

I stripped down and walked into the exam room. I joined a crowd of about a hundred men there. The exam room took up the whole floor, discounting the changing room and lockers. The walls were a stark lime color, and monotonous pale blue linoleum covered the floor.

Male nurses checked my blood pressure, pulse rate, temperature and hearing, and had me do a 360-degree turn-around to see if there were any open sores. I did a squat with my legs, to the floor and back up. I did a pushup, and touched my toes, bending at the waist with my knees locked.

"Any physical disabilities?" one of the male nurses asked me.

"No."

"Excused! Get dressed back up in your clothes. Leave the keys in the lockers. You're free to go."

On the way out I asked a male nurse how I did. He looked at my folder and told me I'd passed with flying colors. He said I would probably be drafted in six months, or sooner.

It felt like my heart fell to the floor. I got dizzy. I grabbed the back of a chair to steady myself, and watched the room spin in front of my eyes. It was like I was watching a carnival carousel go around.

The nurse laughed out loud. I felt my cheeks catch fire.

I'd love to have knocked him right off his chair, but I didn't try.

At first, I didn't tell Kathy. I didn't tell anybody. I was in denial. Talk about falling into a trap. They had me coming and going, I thought.

I knew that if I were drafted, my employer would re-hire me. The "Soldiers' and Sailors' Civil Relief Act of 1940" had guaranteed that since WWII, but it was no consolation.

I waited a few days and then got around to telling Kathy. I waited until after we celebrated Valentine's Day, 'cause I didn't want to ruin her mood.

When I told her, that Sunday, she put both hands up to her cheeks, screamed like I never heard her do before, and then started crying.

She was in a funk from then on, at least until I went to Boot Camp.

We went over to my folk's house after I broke the news to her. I wanted to tell everybody the same day.

Mom, Dad, and my sister, Susan, each took the news differently.

Kathy and I told mom first. She took Kathy in her arms, hugged her tight, whispered, "We'll take care of you, honey," and then looked at me like I'd just been caught cheating on Kathy.

Next, we told dad. He didn't think it was such a big deal. "I guess it was inevitable," he muttered. He went back to watching a football game on TV. Dad never was in the service and I know he must have felt uneasy talking about it with me, or anyone else, for that matter.

My announcement went completely over Susan's head. Being all of sixteen, her life was all about school, her friends, and enjoying life. I don't think she had a clue what the "draft" was.

During dinner, I told my family, "I'm going to enlist instead of waiting for them to draft me. The sooner I get this over and done with, the sooner I can get back on track."

No one said so, but I think they thought I was wacko in the head.

The following Monday, at work, I told my boss, Ed Kam. He was Chinese-Hawaiian about fifteen years my senior. He and I were good friends, both at work and afterward.

"Maybe I could get you to make up a work-related deferment."

Ed just smiled at me and said, "You don't work for a defense-related industry."

He went on to say that since I was eventually going into the service, the company would suspend any of my raises or promotions. He said I would be welcomed back with open arms and that my salary would be adjusted then.

I tried being logical about it. I made up a "wish list."

I didn't want to be in the service for more than two years.

I wanted to be as far away from Vietnam as possible.

I wanted to get in and get out as quickly as possible.

I'd love to work with computers. If I could be assigned a computer job, I could stay up-to-date with data processing.

I could teach self-defense.

Maybe. Maybe. Maybe.

I asked my instructor Ed Parker if he would write me a reference letter about my Kenpo-Karate skills. He did, and I was most grateful. Parker was known as the father of American Kenpo and an international contender.[10]

Ed Kam and our IBM Consultant each wrote me reference letters, too.

I took the next Saturday off from Karate practice and made the rounds with the recruiters. I went to the Coast Guard first. I heard you could enlist with them for six months active, seven-and-a-half years' reserve.

"That program is long gone, bud!" the Coast Guard told me.

The Air Force was next. "Sorry, we only offer four year enlistments."

I approached the Army. "Three years active, three years reserve and the earliest we could take you is October."

I was running out of options!

I went to the Navy recruiter as a last resort. As it happened, he shared an office with a Marine Corps recruiter. The Navy offer was pretty much like the Air Force; four years on and two years reserve. I could go with them in about three months.

The Marine Corps recruiter had been waiting for us to finish talking and asked me to talk to him before I left.

He was a good-looking guy, about my age. He wore a Marine Corps dress blue uniform with stripes on his sleeves, and ribbons and medals on his chest. He was built like a pro wrestler. In a deep, soft voice he said, "Tell me a little about you. Maybe there's something the Corps can offer you."

I took the bait.

---

[10] He passed away in 1990 I'm told. His dojo was later to host such celebrities as Steve McQueen and even Elvis Presley. Source: Kempo/Kenpo FAQ, http://www.urbin.net/EWW/MA/KF/

The Marine told me my letters were impressive, that the Corps always looked for a few good men, that they had computers, so maybe I could be a programmer.

Then he hit me with the clinchers: they had a two year active duty, four year inactive reserve program, and I could go in almost right away. He said, "I'll take your letters of reference and put them right on top of your paperwork. That way it's the first thing they'll see when they open your file."

I gave him my stuff and signed up.

What a stupid thing I've just done, I thought, but there was no turning back.

That was March 10th, 1966. My orders were to report for active duty April 12th.

My life was in turmoil. I guess I quit trying to find a way out of the draft. It seemed like there was no light at the end of my tunnel.

Now that I was headed for the Corps, I began rationalizing it.

I told myself all kinds of erroneous thoughts.

I was going to "fulfill my patriotic duty," *whatever* that meant, by serving in the United States Marine Corps.

I've always believed that patriots deserved respect. I wanted some respect.

"Maybe," I told myself, "this is all part of some great master plan God has set up for me."

My karate friends threw me a going away party. It was at our house, and over 150 people showed up. Ed Parker was there and stayed most of the night. I felt pretty cool! I had three more days to live as a normal citizen.

Since I didn't know what I was going to do for the Corps after Boot Camp. I couldn't speculate with Kathy about what the future would bring to our lives. We were both weepy those few remaining days before my enlistment started. We told each other "I love you," but there wasn't much else to say.

Finally, it was time for me to go, April 12th, 1966.

Ed Kam picked me up at home and drove me downtown to the Induction Center. He stayed with me until I was called to swear in. We waved goodbye to each other and he took off.

After the induction ceremony concluded, I boarded a gunmetal gray bus and rode from L.A. down the coast toward Mexico. The ride to MCRD (Marine Corps Recruit Depot), San Diego, was a silent one. It was about three hours long, and everyone was nervous about what was going to happen next. I was scared witless.

The rest of my experiences are written in letters I sent home to Kathy and my folks.

My love to everyone,

David.

———————————————

I folded the pages of my letter and stuffed them into an envelope. I closed my eyes and fell into a deep sleep. I was startled awake when the plane landed in Okinawa. I mailed the letter on my way to the temporary barracks I would sleep in until my return flight to 'Nam arrived for me.

Warnecki and I found one another while boarding our plane in Okinawa, and sat together on the way back. He said he partied by himself the whole seven days. "I don't remember leaving the hotel one time!" he bragged. We didn't speak to each other after that.

Will this trip to the company be anything like the one I took when I first got to 'Nam? If I only knew then what I know now.

To kill time, and to see if my fractured memory could manage coherent recollection, I went through the first few days of my overseas tour of duty.

I left for Okinawa, Japan on October 16th, 1966. I boarded a Continental Airlines plane and flew from California to Okinawa. We stopped to refuel on Oahu, Hawaii. It was a grueling twenty-hour trip. They fed us two meals

Marine boot camp graduation photo of David W. Powell. Source: DWP

There were two distinctly different groups of men on Okinawa. There were men like us, fresh from the States, terrified about what was to come, and the others, who had finished their 'Nam tour and were elated to be going home. We wasted the days doing nothing, and drank beer at night in the enlisted men's club.

October 20th came around, and I took off for Da Nang, Vietnam. It was on another Continental airplane. Just like the bus to Boot camp had been quiet, the plane ride was silent and the tension in the passenger section was tactile. We flew another ten hours on that 1,500 mile leg.

Believe it or not, they had stewardesses on board, even though it was a military charter flight. When we started to land, I saw the frightened looks on the stewardesses' faces as we approached, ready to land. "They've been here, before, I'll bet!" I said to the guy next to me. Little did I know, I would find out why in less than an hour.

We landed and got off the plane. We moved off the airfield at a slow run. I hadn't reached the edge of the runway before the plane took off again.

The base was the size of a small city of about 4,000 people. Mostly Air Force and Marine Air Command were stationed there. There was no vegetation left anywhere inside the wired perimeter.

I found the mess hall and got something to eat. I found a sleeping area with an empty rack. I asked a Sergeant what was going to happen next.

"You'll be shipping out tomorrow."

"Where can I get a drink?"

"Over there at the club." He pointed to a building to his right.

I had finished my third beer when a Marine burst into the club, shouting "Incoming! Incoming!"

Rockets exploded on the airfield! I freaked out!

"What should I do? What the heck should I do?"

"Get out of here and find a trench to hide in!"

"Boom! Boom! Boom!" rang through my eardrums as the rockets exploded.

I tore out of the club and dived chest first onto the ground.

Within five minutes, "All Clear!" was repeated down the airfield.

I snuck out of the trench and crept onto a cot and stifled my terror as best I knew how.

The next day, I got on another plane and flew to Chu Lai, which was about an hour south of Da Nang. When I got there, it was raining hard, and nonstop.

"D" company was located deep in the jungle. Two other men were going to the same company. They were both friendly kids, recent high school graduates, and ready to fight.

On the trip there, we were drenched to the bone from the non-stop rain. We traveled for three days on trucks, a boat, and by foot. Along the way we stayed overnight at various headquarters.

In Da Nang, the buildings had wooden floors made out of shipping planks, plywood sidings, screens for windows, and ply board roofs. As we went further in country, the quarters gradually became more primitive, culminating in thrown-up tents, without floors, and two-seater latrines for every hundred men.

One night we stayed at Regimental Headquarters. The Chaplain there talked with us for a bit, said a prayer about "doing the very best we can'" while we served our country, and wished us a nice night's sleep. The Father was a tall man, maybe six-two, and was in reasonable physical shape. This was the same chaplain whom I would later watch die in front of me during Operation Rio Blanco.

We went to sleep with the lights on and woke up early the next day. We talked about last night's prayer and wondered why there wasn't any mention of us staying safe, or living through the war we were about to face. We decided that we would be doing plenty of praying for our own safety and our own lives in the coming months.

The next stop was at some company's office. It wasn't "D" company, so I didn't care what it was called. We sat outside the office on a kind of porch with a tarp for a roof. I noticed something out of place just in front of the door. I saw what looked like a toy, green snake.

"Hey! There's a green toy that looks like a snake out here."

A Sergeant stepped out to see what I meant. He had been in country for a few months. I thought I could tell that because he walked slump-shouldered, like there was a heavy load on his back, and was reluctant to make eye contact with me.

"Where's the toy?" he asked.

"There, just under the step going into the office."

He pushed me backward a little, his hand pressed on my chest. "Don't move a muscle. That's a real Bamboo Viper!"

He called to someone in the office and asked for his rifle. Using the barrel of the rifle, he prodded the snake off the beam it was on, and onto the wooden deck. In a flash, he grabbed the rifle barrel, turned the rifle butt-end down, and smashed the snake into two pieces.

"We call them 3-steppers, 'cause if they bite you, you'll be paralyzed in three paces!"

There are no safe times, nor safe places, I thought to myself

We got our field gear at Battalion Supply on our last day of travel. They gave me an M14 rifle, three new, empty rifle magazines, a helmet, two canteens, a cartridge belt, and flak jacket.

"Pick up that helmet over in the corner. You can have that," the Supply Clerk said. He was skinny and wore thick glasses.

I picked up the helmet and looked at it. "You expect me to wear a helmet with a bullet hole in it?" He looked at me sheepishly and gave me a better one.

The flak jacket he handed me was also repulsive. It had dried blood-stains covering half the back panel. I refused it, too.

It was dusk when we finally got to the company hill. We were assigned different tents that would be 'home' for us for the next seven months. Although I'd traveled with two other men since Da Nang, I felt like I was alone.

I came out of my reverie and realized I was still flying back from R&R to 'Nam. I shook my head a few times, left to right, right to left, to clear the cobwebs in my mind.

Warnecki, the other men and I, landed in Da Nang, just like before. Warnecki and I continued on to Chu Lai.

Here we go again!

The Devil brought me back to reality. When we stopped at Division headquarters, we were told to "kick back" and wait for a ride back to our company. Warnecki and I leaned against a wooden building and sat on our haunches, waiting for a ride. Curiosity got the better of him and he peered into the building we were resting against.

"You won't believe this!"

"Believe what?" I retorted.

"Check this out!"

I got up and walked to the door that he had opened. I looked inside and saw a sad, gruesome sight. There were over a hundred black bags, zipped up and closed, that held the bodies of some of my fellow combatants. They were stacked on top of one another, like cords of firewood. Our "rest stop" was "D" Medical, an interim morgue.

Once you're dead, nobody cares what happened to your corpse! You're worthless to the greater mission, so you get pushed out of the way.

I was back in 'Nam. My heart was broken, again. My brain told me that I should cry for those poor men lying on the ground, in those ugly sacks, but there were no tears in my bloodshot eyes.

Warnecki and I shuffled over to another building. We said nothing to one another. We stared at the ground until our first truck ride arrived.

We caught a ride back to Regimental headquarters and then to Battalion headquarters.

We made our way back to the company, which was three-day trip. We were unarmed all the way back to the hill. I wanted a rifle in the worst way!

When we got to the company office a clerk stopped us. Our companies, Bravo and Delta, had gone on another operation and weren't expected back for another few days.

We were given maintenance chores to fill out the days, and bunker watches to fill up the nights. I went out to my tent, against orders, and picked up my rifle and magazine belt. I refused to be unarmed in 'Nam if I had any opportunity to have a weapon.

7 An Office in Hell

Four men had permanent jobs in the company office. They didn't have to go out of the company lines and participate in any combat activities.

There was the Gunny, a sergeant, and two other men, each of them a corporal. I'd met the Gunny in the field. He'd been on the supply truck that was ambushed, where I'd watched "Bear" die.

He'd led a team of riflemen back to the ambush site and captured two of the VC. One of the VC was the prisoner I'd kicked in the face. The Gunny had pulled me aside that day and told me not to do that *ever again*. He then shook my hand and patted me gently on my back.

Gunny had been wounded in the process of capturing them, and was awarded the Purple Heart and Bronze Star medals for his heroism. He was the office "boss." The sergeant was the "supervisor" and as such decided what the others would work on each day.

One of the corporals was assigned the duties of a clerk-typist. He made entries in the Service Record Books of the men in the company, and composed a Daily Unit Diary for headquarters. The other office clerk took care of the incoming and outgoing mail, and other miscellaneous duties.

I envied them. I wanted to be in their shoes, instead of going into battle every day. The clerk-typist was a man named Jenkins. I recognized him as one of the men I had met and served with in boot camp. He looked exactly the same as he did when we graduated. He was healthy and had a relaxed countenance. If he hadn't spent his whole tour in the "rear," excluded from combat, he would have been as wound up as Warnecki and me.

More importantly, Jenkins was a week away from finishing his tour of duty. Jenkins told me that his brother, who joined the Army when he was sent to 'Nam, had orders to go to Saigon. He said the US government policy was to have only one family member in country, and he elected to return home and let his brother serve his country, too. All this didn't matter to me, all I knew was that I had a chance to get out of the field and finish my tour on safer ground.

I chummed it up with him for a half-hour and asked him to show the Gunny my Service Record Book, illustrating my high aptitude scores.

"Could you put in a good word for me? See if they'll consider reassigning me to take your place!"

He said he'd be glad to, but he couldn't guarantee any success. The Sergeant approached me later that day, while I was picking up litter around the office. He asked me if I could still use a typewriter.

"You bet I can, Sergeant!" He gave me a typing test and I managed to average twenty-eight words per minute. He told me that if I wanted a reassignment, I could replace Jenkins and finish my tour working in the company office.

"Hurray!" I shouted.

When the company returned from the field, the Gunny spoke with my platoon leader, Lieutenant Spivey, about my transfer.

I disliked Spivey. He was a tall, thin man and was "full of himself" because he was an officer. Spivey was all of 23 years old, but had a baby face. He had a nasty trait. Occasionally, he snuck up on me, from behind, when I stood night watch. He did that four or five times, and each time it scared me senseless. This added another spike in my already high startle response.

His antics caught up with him eventually and he paid a heavy price for his foolishness. We were on a company-sized operation. It was nighttime and we had set up our perimeter of defense on top of a wooded hill. A machine gun team had been positioned a few meters to my right. They had taped a hand grenade to a tree and strung fishing wire through the firing pin and then secured the other end to an adjacent tree. It was mounted chest-high.

Spivey snuck up on those men, in an attempt to surprise them, and tripped the booby trap. It exploded and severely wounded him on the right side of his head. He was Medivac'ed. The Gunny later read us a letter written from the hospital saying he had been blinded; he never returned to the hill.

My transfer was granted. I picked up the rest of my gear from my tent, promoted my A-Gunner to Gunner, and made a home for myself behind a wall that separated the office from my new living quarters. It was May 21st, 1967, a date I would never forget.

I wouldn't have to go out on patrols anymore. I wouldn't have to go out on operations anymore. No more standing watch at night. That's when I started having nightmares about my combat experiences.

When I transferred from the field and into the company office, what I expected to happen didn't happen. I thought I would be greeted with cynicism for leaving the combat zone behind. Instead, the men I had stood shoulder-to-shoulder with in combat treated me exactly the same, whether I was "Grunting it out" with them on a patrol or handing them their mail from the front door of the company office. I realized that there had been a unique bond established between men who have risked their lives in the same venue.

I value this bond, and will cherish it for the rest of my time here on Earth. Sharing what little we had with each other was a part of that union of spirits. If one man had coffee and the other didn't, the cup would be passed back and forth without a word being spoken.

This sharing sometimes took bizarre turns, like the night a machine gunner I had served with sent a "runner" to my quarters at about 9:00 pm. I didn't know the guy who came to get me, but he said "Andy (not his real name) told me to get you to come with me to his bunker. Don't ask questions. Just follow me, Corporal."

I knew Andrew and trusted him. I followed the courier back to a bunker down the left side of the hill. Inside the bunker were Andy and another Marine I didn't know. They were taking turns raping a young Vietnamese woman.

"Powell! I was never selfish with you in the field, and you'd give me the last bullet you had if I asked you for it. Have some of this ass before I blow her away!"

What has this world of mine come to? Do I even know this man?

"Thanks, but no thanks. I appreciate the offer, but I'll be court-martialed if I'm caught out here, doing that, and I can't risk it. What are you going to do with her after you are done?"

"Take her back outside the wire where we found her and grease her. She's a VC Nurse we caught coming back to the hill. She had this coming for a long time."

I grunted my understanding, and then headed back to my cot thinking about the world I was living in and hating every minute of it.

I didn't make friends with anyone I served with in combat. If I did, (I thought) then I'd worry about them, and if I got distracted like that, either I'd be killed or wounded, or they would be. So, why make friends?

There were many injuries we suffered on a daily basis, from gunshots, land mines, Punji stakes, and booby traps. Somehow, it was easier to accept if it happened to someone I didn't know. I thought friendships would jinx my chances for survival.

I decided that if I got close to someone, I'd begin to worry about their safety. If that happened, the chances were greater that I wouldn't stay focused on saving my own life, and that was not an option for me.

One of my worst experiences actually happened *after* I was assigned to the company office. While I was still in the field, I made a fateful mistake and it cost me dearly, emotionally.

I had returned from a routine patrol early one afternoon. There was a "New Guy" in our tent. He was about nineteen years old. He wore a pale green tee shirt and red Marine Corps swimming trunks.

I looked at him and thought Oh boy, is this guy an innocent, or what?

He returned my stare, gave me a nervous grin, with no teeth showing through his lips. I smiled back.

"Who are you?"

"My name is Kenny Haas. I'm a machine gunner and I just got here."

The latter was obvious. I laughed out loud and said "No kidding, Sherlock!"

Kenny Haas with his M60 machine gun. Source: DWP

I told him my name and that I was with Rockets, showed him around the tent, and assigned him a cot of his own. After he settled in, I gave him a guided tour of the hill so he would know the basics of living there with his and me other tent mates.

Kenny was a very sweet, gentle giant, and I liked him immediately. I took him under my wing and began worrying about his safekeeping while he was in 'Nam.

I knew, however, I'd made a cardinal mistake, for I'd vowed to never make friends in 'Nam.

He had been raised on a farm in Wisconsin along with a passel of siblings. He was used to all sorts of manual labor. Kenny was strong!

One of the daily tasks we did for our tent was to fill four five-gallon cans from a "Water Buffalo," a small tanker towed by the supply truck. We used the water for drinking, shaving, bathing, and cooking.

The Buffalo was two hundred meters up the hill. We'd fill the cans, and carried them back to the tent. Until Kenny showed up, we needed two men to carry the water. Kenny's first turn to get water came up. He grabbed all four cans, got the water, and carried them back. A gallon of water weighs around eight pounds so he had about 160 pounds under his arms. He did the work of two men without the slightest hesitation.

Kenny and I became very close. One day, with no patrols for either of us, he started an intimate conversation. "David. You've become a father-like figure to me. Would you please tell me about how you grew up? I'd really like to know more about you."

"Kenny, sure I will, but I'd like to know how you grew up, first. Tell me about your upbringing."

"OK… but there's not much to tell. I'm one of eight kids, the third one born. I have two younger brothers, ages 5 and 6, and the rest are girls. We all live on the family farm and raise cows for milking. From as long as I can remember I helped dad with the chores. I never went to school. Mom gave all of us the schooling she thought we needed to get by in the world. I enlisted in the Corps when Bobby, my younger brother could take over my family chores. That's me, in a nutshell."

I nodded and thanked him for his history, albeit short and simple. I hadn't thought carefully about my younger days before.

"There's not much to tell you about. I was born and raised in Southern California. I lived in East L.A., Long Beach, and now I live in Pasadena. I've got a younger sister. I'm married. Dad is in data processing. I was a computer programmer, back in "The World." I thought I was going to be drafted, so I enlisted in the Corps and ended up here in this tent with you."

Kenny thanked me, and then we broke off our conversation and wrote letters home.

With a heavy heart, I now say to you that Kenny's childlike innocence caught up with him.

I had been in the company office about two months. The security of the bridge over the river, separating the villes to our right from Hill 55, became the responsibility of my company. It had sandbag bunkers on both ends, where men would stand watch.

One evening, at dusk, some VC assaulted the bridge and killed two men. One of dead men was Kenny. The other was Lance Corporal Gutierrez. Gutierrez was a young, married Mexican-American from Southern California.

Gunny ordered me to identify Kenny's remains for positive identification, 'cause I knew him best. I abhorred the task, but I agreed to do it.

Kenny had been sitting on top of the bunker during his watch, heating some hot chocolate over a C-ration stove, when the attack occurred.

He was nearly cut in half with an RPG-7 shoulder-operated rocket, much like a LAAW. I collapsed to my knees and began sobbing uncontrollably when they turned back the tarp and showed me my dead "adoptee."

The blood drained from my brain. I vomited… I fainted. I was revived by a Corpsman, who jammed some smelling salts under my nose.

Marines Hurl Back VC Assault

S&S Vietnam Bureau

SAIGON — A Viet Cong platoon attacked a Marine platoon guarding a bridge near Da Nang Saturday and broke through the U.S. perimeter before they were driven back.

U.S. headquarters said two Marines were killed and 14 wounded. A Marine platoon usually has about 40 men.

Headquarters said the Communist troops broke through the U.S. defenses in two places and destroyed two bunkers with rockets.

The enemy escaped, apparently taking any casualties with them. There was no report on whether the bridge, 12 miles northwest of Hoi An, was destroyed or damaged.

I had hounded Kenny, constantly, to be vigilant and to protect himself at all times. He forgot, I guess. Maybe he was daydreaming about a happy time in his past. I hope so. How horribly ironic it was that he was killed with a weapon similar to the one I carried when I was in the field.

Lance Corporal Kenneth Daniel Haas (MOS 0331, "Machine Gunner"), formerly of Stanley, Wisconsin, died on August 5th, 1967 at the age of 21 years, The Combat Area Casualties File lists his cause of death due to "fatal injury by an explosive device" and duly notes that his body was recovered.

A few weeks had passed since Kenny died and as the mail was being readied for handout, I came across an envelope addressed to "Anybody who knew Kenneth Haas." I was surprised and bewildered. I took the letter out of the stack and stuffed it into my shirt.

This letter is addressed to me. If anyone knew Kenny well, I was first on that list.

After my shift was over I went over to my cot and sat down. I pulled the envelope out of its hiding place and carefully opened it. The letter began:

Dear friend of Kenneth,

I hope that you can tell us just anything about what happened to my son. Please.

I have asked the Marines about what happened to him, but all they say is that he died in action in Vietnam, and nothing more. We already knew that after they delivered the news and his Purple Heart on our doorstep that horrible day.

Just anything at all you can tell us would be very much appreciated.

Thank you,

Kenneth Haas' Mother

I was touched by the simple request, and enraged at the Corps for being so callous about the death of a loved one. I decided to write her a letter that would praise her son, although Kenny had died probably without ever knowing what hit him or that he was in a firefight. I told her that he fought bravely to defend the bridge. In my heart, I know he would have given it his all anyway, if allowed half a chance. Dead is still dead, valiant or no and I just wanted his mom to be proud or at least feel that he died for something.

On September 18th, 1967, Mrs. Haas wrote back to me.

Dear David,

You will never know how much your letter has ment [sic] to us and that men like you will write such letters trying to comfort us when you men need comforting too. I have heard of the deep friendships that these soldiers make and keep. I don't know quite how, but it seems you have answered our questions without us ever asking them. It did his father good to hear how Kenneth talked of farming as Kenneth was the one who could do the most work of the three oldest boys. Since you wrote to us we have received letters from LCPL David Barclay, Jerry Shehan, and Roy Sprague.

I want to tell you how wonderful I think you boys must be with the fear and hardships and so seldom a word wrote home about them. Only now can I guess at what it must be like to live in this danger and fear. How I wish I might help in some small way.

I just got a call from Minneapolis that they have four medals to present to us. The Purple Heart is one. It is hard to receive them. During our bad time, Kenneth's two older brothers came home and helped were [sic] ever they could, wash dishes, cook, clean, and help Dad with the two little brothers. So please say a few prayers for Kenneth, seven brothers and sisters and a Mom and Dad too.

May god bless you and keep you.

Kenneth's mother
Mrs. Melburn Haas
Stanley, WI, RR1

Life, in "the rear," was infinitely safer. There were no more patrols, no watch to stand, and no more surprise operations to go on. Still, I carried my rifle and ammunition every time I ventured out of the office.

Sergeant Laulu wandered into the office one afternoon. He asked if he had any mail lately. He said he hadn't heard from his family in over three weeks and thought that his letters got hung up in the "system." I told him "No, Sarge, there isn't any undelivered mail for you here. (In retrospect, that was a clue that the folks in the "real world" were distancing themselves from us warriors.)

I asked Laulu why I didn't get a Purple Heart the day we were ambushed. He said, "I remember the Corpsman patched you up, Powell. How bad were you wounded?"

"Not bad. He rubbed some alcohol over my chest with a cotton swab. My flak jacket absorbed most of the impact, and left me with a little cut across the left side of my ribcage."

"I guess he was paying you back for killing that woman, or something like that. Doc didn't like you very much. I knew he didn't put you in for it, on purpose, but I was waiting to see if you'd ask me about it." He turned around, faced the Gunny, and told him about the incident.

Receiving my Purple Heart (07/06/1967). Source: DWP

The Gunny was angry! "[Expletive]! I'll tell the Captain and get this taken care of, Powell. I'm sorry you were disrespected."

I had been working in the company office for six weeks when Gunny's time in country expired. A First Sergeant (nickname: Top) was assigned to replace him and took command of the company office. He was short and fat. I was happy to see the Gunny get out of Vietnam, yet sad at the same time because he was a good man and I'd miss his friendship.

Top had been transferred to Vietnam, and to our company, for something he must have done terribly wrong back in the States. I say that because he had been a Tuba player in the Marine Corps Band prior to replacing Gunny.

Until his arrival, I enjoyed a modicum of respect for my service in the field. The respect came from the Gunny and the other office men, as well as the men still in the field that knew me. This treatment was horrendously dashed after the Top found out that I was an Infantryman, first, and not a "legitimate" administrative aid. He threw a fit when he reviewed my Service Record Book and saw I was a Grunt.

"What are you doing working in the office! You belong in the field! As soon as another admin man shows up anywhere in the Battalion, he's going to replace you and you're going back where you belong!"

The Top was a cruel, vicious boss. He began every morning the same way. As soon as he strode into the office he would shout out my last name, then issue the same threat.

"Powell!", he bellowed.

"Yes, First Sergeant!"

"Any admin men here yet?"

"No, First Sergeant!"

"Then get to work and find me one!"

I loathed him. I thought he had the authority to send me back to face the dangers that patrols and operations posed. I was scared out of my mind. His abuse of me greatly enhanced my fear and resentment of authority figures.

The Battalion officers finally realized the significance of the problems with the M16 and subsequently had a makeshift firing range constructed about a hundred meters to the rear of my office. It was put in between the office and the mess hall. It was built just below "street level," which muffled the sporadic gunfire noise.

An admin man showed up at the company in late August. The Top was grinning ear-to-ear! "Get ready to pack up, Powell!"

Instead of replacing me in the company office, he took over Top's duties in the office. This sat well with the Top, but it also proved that the officers in my company had more authority than he did. The Top discontinued his daily taunts, but his smirk whenever he looked at me continued the mental abuse. He also quit coming into the office on a daily basis.

I took the new man over to the mess hall for lunch. We were walking side-by-side, chatting about nothing in particular, when we passed by the rifle range. Suddenly, a few men shot several semi-automatic rifle bursts on the range. I instinctively dived to the ground. The sergeant just stood there looking at me with a wide-eyed stare and a smile across his face. I was humiliated! My startle-response reaction was seared even deeper into my subconscious.

In October 1967, I decided to take another R&R. I chose not to go visit with Kathy, based in part upon how the visit had gone when I did see her, and in part based upon how I felt about her after I received those repetitious letters from her. She never quit writing me about her fun times at night and on weekends. I felt like she had been cheating on me!

I was introduced to Kathy via a "blind date." I'd loved Kathy before all this combat stuff, but I had lost that love for her and for my fellow humans, and for myself.

After our first date, Kathy gave me her address and telephone number. To say that we hit it off right away was an understatement.

She had spent the first fourteen years of her life on Oahu, Hawaii before moving to Alhambra, California. Her family consisted of three brothers, a little sister, herself, and her mom and dad. Her dad was self-employed as a cabinetmaker and made a nice, modest living for all of them.

Probably her best quality was her honesty. She couldn't tell a lie, even if it was going to hurt her in the long run. In the end, her "honest" letters *did* hurt her.

Since Kathy was Hawaiian and I had a Hawaiian Karate instructor, I bragged about my prowess. I invited her to watch me teach an intermediate class some evening. When she showed up one night I introduced her to Mr. Parker, my Hawaiian-born instructor. They got along great; talking in "Pigeon English" like old school chums. This affinity she had with Mr. Parker encouraged me to study karate in earnest.

Kathy and I married just before I turned twenty-two. We were supposed to go on our honeymoon at the beaches of Southern California for two weeks. My employer at the time asked me to reconsider this vacation and honeymoon.

They told me that if I took just one week of time off, instead of two, I would be promoted to "computer programmer," given a nice raise, and would start out on a new vocation.

I was given a career choice and I accepted the offer, over the tears and pleadings of my brand new wife. My new position required a considerable amount of my time, but it was easy and fun to do, and being a programmer became my primary vocation for many years to follow.

Kathy and I tried to have kids right after we were married, but we found out that it would take a miracle for her to get pregnant. She had a medical condition they called something like "Endometriosis."

All that history with Kathy was contained in another lifetime.

I went on R&R to Japan. I stayed in a little town outside of Tokyo. I didn't want the crowds or the "hustle-bustle" of big city life. The R&R lasted seven days. The day before I was scheduled to return, I took a tour offered by the hotel where I stayed. The tour went by train to and from a large lake. Other servicemen were in the travel party.

The sights were beautiful but the train ride back to the hotel area was horrible and mysterious. When the tour group started back to the train station from the boat landing, the tour guide told us all to run to the station as fast as we could. No one stopped to ask why; we took off and didn't stop until we were on the train.

I asked the tour guide, after the train started back down the tracks, why we had to run like that.

"War protesters were headed toward our group, and I didn't want you folks to be exposed to their antics."

That was the first glimpse I had that the participants in the Vietnam War were unpopular. I went back to Hill 55 and finished my tour, and wondered what kind of reception awaited me back "in the World."

Thoughts about my in-country service haunted my days and nights as I waited to go home. They intruded on my sleep in the form of nightmares. My comrades scared me.

On the morning of November 7th, 1967, I stood in a roughly thrown-together formation with other men waiting to go home. We were on the Da Nang airstrip. A ground crew put our gear onto a baggage cart and drove toward the cargo hold of the airplane that would take us home.

Aghast, I watched the cart operator/idiot run into the front wheel housing of the plane. The civilian aircrew declared the plane too hazardous to transport us to Okinawa. It flew off empty, except for the crew.

The accident meant that I had to spend another rotten day in Vietnam. A couple of us went for a walking tour of Da Nang "city" that afternoon. We strolled around like tourists. It was all very interesting and fun for us until we noticed that it was getting dark, fast.

We finished returning to the air base at a full run, looking over our shoulders to see if we were going to get attacked.

The next day, another airplane came and finally took me to Okinawa. I picked up my orders, withdrew five-hundred bucks of back pay from my account, went out on the town for a few drinks, returned to the barracks, claimed a bunk bed for my own, and got ready to go to sleep.

To be on the safe side, I hid my wallet between the mattress and springs. I had about four hundred bucks left. The next morning my wallet was nowhere to be found. My own men had robbed me!

Later that day I was on a plane heading stateside. With a fuel stop on Guam, and another on Oahu adding to the trip time, we flew for around seventeen hours.

8   Back in the USA

> "I wish I had things in as good shape in the United
> States as you have here."
> —Lyndon B. Johnson to General Westmoreland
> in Cam Rahn Bay, Vietnam address, Dec. 23rd, 1967

Finally, on the morning of November 10th, 1967, we were in the airspace over El Toro Marine Corps Airbase, some fifteen miles up the Southern California coast from Camp Pendleton. As I understood later, we landed at El Toro Airbase for a reason. Landing at a civilian facility would have subjected embarrassment, mental and physical abuse, and us departing veterans to ridicule. Think about the incidents where vets were spat upon in 1967 and forward.

For the next two hours, the plane circled the landing strip, and then finally landed. All the men aboard the flight wondered why we didn't land. When asked, the stewardesses claimed not to know. We found out after we landed.

We were led into a large auditorium and ordered to sit down. A short, stocky Gunnery Sergeant, gravely attired in his dress blues uniform, hollered the answer we wanted.

He asked for volunteers to greet President Johnson, whose arrival at the base had delayed our landing until Air Force One landed![11]

"Raise your hand and be counted!" he bellowed.

No hands went up. The Gunny made a telephone call, presumably to his superior. After he hung up the phone, he then told the group that all volunteers would be allowed to go on their leave before the rest of us would be let go.

Fifty-some men raised their hand. When the volunteers left the auditorium, the rest of us were immediately processed for leave, while the poor

---

[11] "Public May Greet LBJ at El Toro", *LA Times*, Nov. 10th, 1967. pg. OC8

suckers who had volunteered stood in an adjacent room, waiting for the President to disembark!

Will they ever stop lying to me?

I went on a twenty-day leave in the United States before being transferred back to Camp Pendleton, where it all started. Kathy was there to meet me. She waited outside the auditorium.

There was no chill-down period. Going from either killing or being killed in 'Nam to going out to dinner with my wife, in one twenty-four hour period, seemed a more than a little unfair to her. And it was!

I felt like I was the "Prom King," about to go to my High School graduation dance! Alas, there wasn't any jubilation when I got home. The women in my life gave me hugs of short duration; the men limply shook my hand. I felt like they were ashamed of me, rather than proud of my contributions to our country as a war veteran.

I weighed 133 pounds, having lost 20% of my body weight during the thirteen months of my tour. I was exhausted and weak. I felt like I had struggled for two years and ended up empty-handed, disrespected, and unloved.

Kathy worked days at the beauty salon, which left me with plenty of solitary time to reflect on what had happened to me. Before my enlistment I was a mature young man, successful in his social life. I was happily married, had a good job working with leading-edge computer technology, earning good money, was relatively debt-free, was practicing a new-to-America martial art (Kenpo Karate) and was excelling in it, had a few close friends, and was very self-assured.

After Boot Camp, ITR (Infantry Training Regiment), and AIT (Advanced Infantry Training), I had retained my physical and mental prowess. After my tour of duty in Vietnam, I felt physically inferior and mentally shattered. Some of the emotional wounds I had incurred were thinly scabbed over, but other ones still lay bare.

Ironically, a month after my leave ended, President Johnson swooped into Cam Ranh Bay, Vietnam for a surprise Christmas 1967 visit to rally the troops[12]. Before an audience of 2,500 troops he said, "The enemy knows he has met his master in the field."

I returned to Camp Pendleton, California to serve out the remaining six months of my two-year enlistment. Having been a clerk-typist for the previous six months of my tour served me well, again. The Captain of 'D' company when I left 'Nam thought very highly of me and gave me a proficiency rating of 4.9; perfect is 5.0.

The company I joined at Pendleton, "L" company, gave me the title and responsibilities of Chief Clerk, Company Office. This position meant that I would be excused from any field maneuvers, rifle inspections, and other grunt work as my active duty enlistment expired.

In an odd coincidence, I found that a friend from Advanced Infantry Training (AIT), way back when, was in "K" company at Pendleton. That AIT training session was more than a year ago but it seemed like another lifetime.

He was a clerk in their company office. His name was Hamilton. Hamilton was a year or two younger than me. He had never seen any combat. He seemed genuinely happy to be a Marine, contrary to my opinion of the Corps. Hamilton was an average-looking man and was very talkative.

He was married to a woman named Helen and lived in El Monte, close to Pasadena, and he had a car on base. Nightly, he and I drove home to spend the evenings with our wives. We also spent the weekends at home, away from the Corps.

I renewed my connections with my previous employer and expressed my desire to come back to work after mustering out.

The Marine Corps wanted me to stay on active duty and re-enlist. I was recommended for a meritorious promotion to Sergeant. Five times. The condition of promotion was that I re-enlist for four years. I would not have any of this, and politely refused each time I was asked.

---

[12] "LBJ Visits Troops", *LA Times*, December 23rd, 1967.

During that time my grandmother, on my father's side of the family, passed away. When I attended the funeral with my family, I wore my Dress Green uniform. During the services, I began to tremble and cry. I thought about all the guys who were killed back in 'Nam. I was embarrassed and did my best to hide my grief. I never went to another funeral again.

The emotional flooding I experienced (trembling, crying, etc.) stayed just below the surface of my mind, though I struggled furiously to control it, for decades.

I left active duty on April 11, 1968. Shortly thereafter, I caught up with Bill White, my only close friend since the age of twelve. He went into the Navy right after we graduated from high school. Bill was a trustworthy friend. We stayed in close contact while he was in the Navy, years before enlistment ever crossed my mind.

Bill had been on active duty for over a year when he decided to get out. He feigned a mental illness, simulating fear and loss of speech. It worked, and they terminated his service with a less-than-honorable discharge. I felt sad for his failure. I knew he didn't want to serve his country any longer, and that was OK with me, because I had no intention of ever going into the military myself.

We remained close, right up until the time I returned home from 'Nam. We were out drinking right after my discharge and he asked me if I killed anyone while I was there.

"Yes. I did."

"How could you? No one could make ME do that!"

"Well, I've done my part for my country, not like you, Bill!"

He stomped out of the bar and out of my life after I said that to him. I stayed and had another drink, reflecting on what had happened a moment before. I also remembered that I had witnessed men Frag themselves to get out of the war.

I thought Bill was no better than they were and let our friendship end, along with the last of my drink for the night.

The before-and-after details of most of my traumatic experiences have faded from my mind. For approximately two years after I returned to civilian life, if someone asked me what happened on a particular day, I could tell him or her in detail.

Every branch of the service except the Marine Corps had a twelve-month tour of duty. The Marine Corps, who knows why, set their tour's length at thirteen months. Nonetheless, it was a fixed tour. I know of no other war that had such a fixed tour of duty.

Coming back from Vietnam in late 1967, and the years that followed, were not good years to have been in the military, fought for my country, and/or tried to be a hero.

In fact, the title "Coward" was used in place of the title "Patriot." The "brave" people, the real "heroes," didn't enter the military service. That's my opinion of what the civilian atmosphere was like when I returned from Vietnam.

Vietnam protests become common on campuses nationwide. Source: Nat'l Archive.

I repressed all of my war experiences. In fact, when I had the choice to do so, I would deny I was ever in the service. I lived in Southern California. I would say I spent the time I was away in Northern California. I used that disguise to avoid confronting the verbal and emotional abuse of having been a Vietnam veteran. God forbid they might've found out that I was a *combat* veteran!

1968 was a very troubling year, as it related to Vietnam veterans. In my opinion, it was one of the worst years. The entire country, it seemed, hated the United States' involvement, and more so the participants.

I was a harmed "child." So were many of my comrades. The citizens of this country for whom I had risked my life did not take that into account. I didn't know it at first, but my mind and ego had been shattered. Actually, I didn't seek help for my plight until 1986, two decades later.

In WWI, WWII, and Korea, the men and women who fought those wars received thanks. They were thanked, then and there, by the whole nation. Not so the Vietnam veteran, despite the parties we've had recently, with names like Operation Welcome Home, in Branson, Missouri, not too long ago[13].

My Vietnam War was a very individualized experience. It had a specific beginning and it had a specific end: thirteen months—three-hundred-and-ninety-seven days. Depending on when the airplane came to take me home, it was that many hours.

The day my foot touched the ground in Vietnam, was the day my "go home" meter began to run. As long as I could keep my feet down on the ground and stay alive, I knew I was going to get out at some point.

Another interesting thing about the Vietnam conflict was that it was a guerilla war—start to finish—all ten years. We'd never fought a guerilla war before: where women, children, old men, old women, anybody who was a Vietnamese citizen could be a Viet Cong whenever they chose to be. Throw a hand grenade, and he or she was a Viet Cong; clean your shirt the next day and he or she was an upstanding Vietnamese citizen.

---

[13] See http://www.operationhomecomingusa.com/ and others

There was no group camaraderie that I experienced. Other Vietnam vets felt differently. Some felt isolated like me, before and after, and in fact avoided ex-vets.

But others forged immensely strong friendships that have lasted, and grouped into associations that campaigned for the recognition of PTSD and received compensation for it, provided mutual support, and looked after each other's families.

For me, there was only jealousy. I was jealous of the New Guy because he didn't know the horrors that lay ahead. I was jealous of the guy who had been there one day before me, because he was going home before me.

Once I stepped my foot down on Vietnam soil, my tour of duty began. That's also the time my war started.

There were rocket attacks on Da Nang. They shot at me from ten miles away. There were mines, booby traps, Punji sticks, ambushes, the North Vietnamese Army, deserters, malingerers, and cowards everywhere.

There was danger from above, from either side of me, from behind my back, from tree lines, from hedgerows, from children, from men and women farmers, from the ground I walked on. Everywhere I looked and everyone around me was dangerous. This went through my mind, nonstop, twenty-four hours a day, for thirteen months.

9 Return to Civilian Life

After my discharge, I went straight back to work for my former manager Ed Kam. Ed and I had become good friends before I'd left and he remained my friend when I came back.

There had been some significant changes inside and outside the data processing department. When I had left to go serve my country, the Accounts Payable manager supervised the department. Mr. Harold was a hands-off, kindly gentleman, who let Ed run his department as Ed saw fit.

Our department now reported to the company Controller, Mr. Grundig. The Controller didn't like Mr. Kam, for reasons I never found out. Grundig let everyone know who was in charge of the data processing department—he was!

Another change affected me dramatically. The IBM 1410 Data Processing System I was familiar with, and knew how to write software programs for, had been replaced by a new IBM system. I didn't know the first thing about how it worked or how to write programs to use on it.

I was two years behind my colleagues. Virtually, I lost my vocation. I was obsolete! I had no idea what my work future would be like, and it scared me to acknowledge that to myself. My military service had cost me two years of good pay and a nice career.

The employees who were still there when I returned to work treated me like a resented teacher's pet. Those who I thought were friends turned out not to be. A gross understatement would have been "The first week back was an unhappy one."

The IBM System/360 computer had the capability of running the old software via emulation. This was inefficient, but it meant that my prior skills would still be of value to the company. I breathed a huge sigh of relief. Maybe *all* was not lost.

It was imperative that I go to school and learn the current programming languages. Ed said that was to be arranged at some later date, but there were enhancements and corrections that needed to be made to the old systems right then.

There were no pay increases because Grundig wanted me to prove my worth to the company first. I didn't know that was his agenda for me.

Three months came and went, like a lightning bolt. Ed Kam and I were called into Grundig's office after my ninety days were up.

Grundig said, "The Soldiers and Sailors Act is only good for ninety days. Since you don't know how to make software for the new computer, you are no longer of any value to the company. Therefore, Mr. Powell, you are fired!"

His words ran threw me like a hot knife through a stick of soft butter. At first, I was speechless. I almost started to cry. Ed saw the state I was in. He tried to stand up for me, but the Controller would hear none of that. Ed stopped talking and looked down at the floor.

I pleaded with Grundig to let me keep my job.

"If you would please send me to school and let me prove to you that I can be productive and valuable to the company, you won't be wrecking my career or my home life."

"You haven't been to the new computer language schools? Ed, is this true?"

"Yes, sir. We needed to make changes to the old programs and I thought Dave could start out...."

"That's enough, Ed. We'll talk about this later. Mr. Powell, you will be given another ninety day probation, after you have completed the language schools that I will enroll you in, myself. You may keep your job until then."

After we left the office, Ed looked over at me as we headed to the parking lot.

"How could you humiliate yourself like that? I would have never begged like you just did! Why'd you tell him I kept you out of school? That was a dirty trick you played on me!"

I didn't answer him. We took off and drove home in different directions. In my car I thought to myself, *Here I go having to take care of myself again, just like in 'Nam. Everybody is a still a threat to my happiness.*

Fortunately, I managed to learn the new computer languages: Assembler, the more difficult to learn because it was written at the machine level, and COBOL, a more English-like language.

I was a very angry man. I stayed angry for many years to follow. This mental state, in my opinion, was a manifestation of my PTSD before I left Vietnam.

I needed some anger management. I decided that, although it had been two years since I'd tried to practice my Karate, I would go back into my self-defense training.

Yet again, there had been quite a bit of material taught to my former Karate classmates in the time I was gone. I was motivated to get back in shape, re-learn some moves that I had forgotten, and catch up.

I got in shape pretty quickly and resumed teaching intermediate classes two nights a week. After the classes ended, my advanced classes began. I was now venting some of my anger, physically, two hours a night, two days a week.

That wasn't enough for me, so I began training six to eight hours every Saturday. In November 1968, after six months of rigorous practice, Mr. Parker promoted me to 1st Degree Black Belt.

I had learned to program the new computer and kept my job, but the work environment was an unhappy one, and after a year there, I looked for a new job.

Kathy and I tried, unsuccessfully, to have children. The primary reasons to have kids were medical ones. She had been diagnosed with having two serious medical conditions. She had Endometriosis, which gave her severe cramps every menstrual cycle. It was thought that if she became pregnant the problem might disappear.

She also had Lupus Erythematosus, known as "Wolf Mask." In 1969, that disease was thought to be terminal, and my parents suggested that children would make her final years happier.

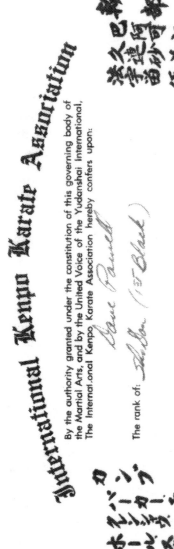

1st Degree Black Belt Certificate.

Kathy and I did not get along. I was still very pained by those letters she'd written to me while I was in the field. As I said before, one of Kathy's faults was her honesty. She didn't give any thought about what I felt as she glowingly told me of her escapades.

If I had not gone into the service, my marriage might have survived.

We struggled to pay the monthly bills, so she went back to work full-time as a cosmetologist. I was still getting paid my 1966 wages. I saw it as my duty to stay with her and try to have children because of her almost certain fatal illness, rather than get a divorce and move out of the house.

My parents, in an attempt to integrate me back into a life-as-usual program, took me to a nine-hole golf course for a July 4th 1968 outing. At the sixth hole that morning, around 8 am, we were all approached the green, ready to putt out.

Someone near the golf course lit off a string of firecrackers in celebration of our Independence Day. The next two things I remember from that episode are: (1) I found myself prone in a sand trap adjacent to putting surface with the business-end of my putter buried in my right shoulder, pointing my would-be "rifle," as it were, toward the origin of the noises, and (2) coming back into real-time and saw both my mom and dad turn 180 degrees away from me, shocked and bewildered at my behavior.

Embarrassed and humiliated, I stood up, tried to brush sand off my clothes with my trembling hands, and broke the stony silence, and announced "Happy Fourth of July!"

Nothing was spoken about my antics then, or ever. Nobody ever asked me the question "What was it like, over there?"

My sister, Susan, graduated from high school and was a Homecoming Princess. Now, based upon the purchase agreement my parents and I had initially agreed to, the house we were living in could be sold and my wife and I could look for one of our own choosing.

We decided to list and sell the Pasadena house. After it was on the market for a few months, she became pregnant. We decided not to sell until after our baby came, but we had just extended our real estate listing for another ninety days, and I couldn't take the house off the market.

An offer to purchase the house was presented to us. I told the broker that we didn't want to sell at this time, because of the pregnancy. The broker said that we should look at the offer anyhow and decide whether the sale would be in our best interests, after all. He went on to say that we could change our minds even if we took the offer, so it would always be our option, right up until the day escrow closed.

It was a reasonable offer, one that was about a thousand dollars more than we asked. I accepted the terms and the escrow proceeded forward. I started to become nervous about moving and handling a newborn at the same time.

I liked to take care of things one at a time. I told the broker that we decided not to sell and asked him to tell the buyer the house was off the market. He said that I had to sell, or the buyer could sue me for breach of contract, which he had conveniently omitted telling me when I accepted the offer. That was another lie, from yet another source I thought I could trust.

Kathy gave birth, and we celebrated the first of two sons. We named our first boy Matthew. He was born healthy and strong.

Kathy's cramps went away with the birth of Matthew. She became pregnant shortly thereafter with our second boy. We chose the name Mark for our next newborn.

The medical community had revised Kathy's diagnosis of Lupus. They discovered that there were two forms of the illness, one being systemic, and the other topical.

Her diagnosis was revised to reflect the topical form, which was not fatal. Yet another "authority figure" had lied to me, in my opinion. My distrust of all authority figures was aggravated.

The reasons Kathy and I stayed together were rapidly disappearing.

Meanwhile, an employment recruiter (headhunter) lined me up with an interview as a Senior Programmer at Union Bank. I got the job, gave notice of my termination to Carnation, and started my new job. I was hopeful I'd make new friends there. This also gave me an opportunity to hide my military service background.

No one at my new job will ever know that I was in the service! I vowed.

In one respect, this was a good move on my part. The pay was better, and there were more interesting assignments. The negative aspect was that I had left a team of four programmers whom I liked.

Now, Kathy and my children and I could afford to buy a new house and pay the monthly bills with my substantially higher paychecks. We found a great home on a cul-de-sac in Arcadia, California, and moved in.

Kathy was now a fulltime homemaker and mother. As my luck would have it, we had money problems again. The kids were costing us more than I thought they would've, and she spent money as if we were still childless.

Her going back to work was not an option, because professional day-care was scarce and expensive. I had to find an evening job to supplement my day job income. I liked working for Union Bank and didn't want to job-hop just to make ends meet.

I started my programming job at Union as a COBOL programmer. I had a warm spot for Assembler, because it was very much like the IBM computer language I had known so well with the older model. The operating system (OS) that ran the Union Bank application programs was written in Assembler.

The Systems Programming section learned that I could write in Assembler and transferred me there, working with one other fellow. Leonard was his name. He was British, not terribly good-looking, and smarter than most men I had worked with before.

Leonard and I got along fine. He was more experienced that I was and taught me advanced programming skills. When a new version of the CO-BOL-68 language came out, we implemented it onto the computers. I then set myself up as the office expert of the new language version, and helped other programmers learn the new features.

Leonard took a night job teaching Assembler at the Computer Learning Center (CLC), in downtown Los Angeles. I told him I was looking for an evening job and he managed to get me hired as an evening COBOL teacher at CLC.

Beginning in 1972, I taught classes three nights a week for two years. The extra pay kept Kathy at home and relieved a good portion of our growing debt. My Karate training came to an end.

After class, Leonard and I would have a few drinks at a bar and grill down the street from CLC before we left for home. By 10 pm the bar was almost deserted on weeknights. The place was divided equally—half barroom, half dining area. We sat in the dining area so we could flirt with the waitresses who worked there.

My sex life at home was non-existent, but I still found attractive women desirable. A new cocktail waitress named Monica started work at the bar. I thought she was pretty and had a nice figure.

After we spent a few months getting acquainted, I asked her out. She knew I was married but nevertheless, accepted my invitation. I had an affair with Monica. The separation from Kathy was a terrible personal loss, and it would not be the only such loss I would suffer as my life edged on. Shortly before our separation I was arrested for drunk driving and was briefly incarcerated (overnight). When I was released and at home the next morning, Kathy asked me, in a sarcastic tone, "What do you want?"

"I want my mind to be free of what I learned in Vietnam. I want to sleep at night, without alcohol numbing my brain. I want to be thanked for fighting in a war. I want to be called a 'Patriot.' I want to be a good father. I want to have someone, anyone, hug me and say 'welcome home; all is forgiven.' I want to have back the innocence I lost in my life so that I can look ahead without distrust. I want to cry… out loud. and not be embarrassed about it. I want my brain to be cleansed. Anything more you want to know?!"

"No! You selfish want-to-be. Go out and be that, but don't make me feel *your pain*, whatever that is!"

She slammed her tiny fist on a countertop and stormed out of the kitchen. I poured myself another glass of Scotch and sat down in our living room, looking at (in my mind's eye) the Vietnam valley that stretched out before me as I sat on the latrine in Chu Lai.

Though I did not know it at that time, my psychological makeup regarding relationships had been severely altered after my Vietnam experiences. I abhorred periods of separation from people close to me:

people I trusted. In retrospect, I attribute this to the feelings I experienced when my "comrades" abandoned me under enemy fire.

I moved out of our house and into Monica's apartment with her and her girlfriend, Betty. I visited with my children every weekend, by myself. After a month or so, Monica became concerned about my being with my wife and kids without her being there. She insisted that I take her the next time I went for my visit, which I did.

We picked up the kids and took them to a nearby park for some play-time outdoors. Several hours passed and it was time to take them back home to their mother. Kathy met us at the door, kissed the children "Hello" and invited Monica and me into the living room. As Monica and I sat on the couch next to each other, the kids called Kathy into another room for something or another. When she returned to the living room, Monica turned my face toward hers and gave me a long, wet, kiss. Infuriated at this spectacle, Kathy demanded that we leave immediately.

When the next time I could visit the kids came around, I called Kathy to arrange a pickup time. She said "I will let you pick them up at my house, as usual, but don't *even think* of bringing that Harlot with you! I never want to see her again!" Monica refused to let me go by myself to see my babies and I was too afraid of losing Monica to go against her. That decision finalized my separation from Kathy and my boys.

In early 1972, Kathy and I divorced. I gave her title to the house with a "quit claim deed," and monthly child support. Monica and I developed a love for each other. We talked a little about my work history and quite a bit about my disdain for the American public.

10 Post Traumatic Stress Disorder

Even though Hồ Chí Minh had died in 1969, the war would rage on for another six years. On January 15th, 1973, citing progress in peace negotiations, Nixon announced the suspension of offensive action in North Vietnam which was later followed by a unilateral withdrawal of U.S. troops from Vietnam.

The Paris Peace Accords were later signed on January 27th, which officially ended U.S. involvement in the Vietnam conflict. However, five days before the peace accords were signed, Lyndon Johnson, whose presidency had been marred by the war, died. The mood during his state funeral was one of intense recrimination because the war's wounds were still raw. However, there was relief that not only U.S. involvement in Vietnam ended, but also a chapter on one of the most tragic and divisive eras in the life of the United States came to a close.

The first American prisoners were released on February 11 and all U.S. soldiers were ordered to leave by March 29. In a break with history, soldiers returning from the Vietnam War were generally not treated as heroes, and soldiers were sometimes even condemned for their participation in the war. The peace agreement did not last[14].

It was now the middle of 1973, and I began having some serious mental and emotional problems. My war with Vietnam was far from over. I had nightmares about my Vietnam experiences frequently, almost nightly. I would wake with a start, trembling and shaking.

I tried self-medication with scotch, gin, wine, and other spirits. Regardless of my level of intoxication, the dreams persisted.

I didn't get drunk during my workdays. If I worked overtime, or taught night school, I postponed my consumption of alcohol until my re-

---

[14] Source: Wikipedia (http://en.wikipedia.org/wiki/Vietnam_War)

sponsibilities had been met. Then I drank until I passed out. I found my way to bed most nights, but occasionally I woke up in the living room.

I found that the more self-abuse with liquor I undertook to relieve my mental suffering and intrusive thoughts, the more they worsened. The "hole" I was in continued to deepen.

I was convicted of DUI (Driving Under the Influence) three times.

After the second conviction, I was court-ordered to attend an "Anger Management" program. I went to the one-on-one sessions with a therapist for a short time. The suggestion was made that if I could manage my bouts of rage without using alcohol to numb my emotions, then my problematic drinking would go away.

The therapist invited me to physically express my anger at a punching bag, rather than hold it in and let it fester and become worse, rather than better. After three meetings where I all-but-destroyed the mock "enemy" with my hands and feet, I was asked to quit the program, never to return. The court was informed that I had undertaken the course as outlined and had accepted the suggested alternative actions for anger management. I think that the therapist was afraid that my expressions of rage would eventually turn away from the punching bag and redirect it toward her.

I didn't use drugs. I was afraid of them because of their illegality, cost, uncertain availability, and I knew I would become an addict, based on my alcohol dependency and cigarette smoking habit. I had nowhere to turn for help. I didn't approach the V.A. for help because I thought they didn't recognize "war trauma" as a service-connected problem. Neither did I.

I was in a constant state of hypervigilance, extra-alert at all times for fear of some unknown attack. I felt very, very vulnerable. I attribute this behavior to having been shot at numerous times.

My distrust of authority figures was exaggerated beyond reason. I abhorred being ordered to do things against my will, stemming in no small part from being ordered to risk my life multiple times in combat. My First Sergeant had *burned into my brain* that people who had a say in my future were capable of being cruel. This was the guy ("Top") who'd kept trying to kick me back into the field.

My exaggerated startle-response caused me immeasurable suffering, to the point of public embarrassment. I became noticeably jumpy at the slightest unfamiliar sound. More than a few times, when an unexpected sound or movement caught my attention, I dived to the ground. Other times my neck would compress and my eyes widened. I found myself prone on a busy street in downtown San Francisco, during lunch hour, three times (at least), still dressed in my business suit. After each instance, I retreated to my apartment, locked the door, stripped naked, and drank myself to sleep. My lame excuses for my absences at work were accepted without question, but with a large amount of unspoken disdain.

I openly wept (another feeling of weakness and shame) when I experienced, or saw, touching exchanges between partners, or the adulation of crowds when athletes performed well.

I felt sorry for myself. I had nowhere to turn for help.

I was convinced that my world was not a safe place to be in and I was angry at it, and the population at large.

I knew that I had a foreshortened lifespan. The wear and tear on my organs from adrenalin surges would eventually kill me at an age younger than my peers.

Whatever I was doing at the present time, I did not want to do. I ran from one situation to another. I practiced avoidance and escape, rather than try to develop and employ healthy coping skills.

Up until the end of 1973, my skills as a data processor would still actively be sought out. "Headhunters" would telephone me at work on a regular basis. They offered me attractive positions with their clientele. I grew to be increasingly susceptible to the temptation to pick up and move along.

A position as programming supervisor at Jackson and Hobbs (Insurance brokers) came my way. I took the interview, then the job that was offered me, in late 1973. After working there for about four months, I realized that they were not interested in the development of new applications for their computer. I was in a dead-end job with no prospect for future growth. Again, it came time to change.

Then, the Headhunter calls ended. I had been labeled a "job hopper," someone who shows up for three or four months then leaves before the deadlines really hit or their work gets scrutinized. My search for new employment was limited to scanning the weekend job classifieds in the local newspapers. By sheer luck, I happened upon a computer consultancy ad that offered overseas employment in Australia.

My PTSD symptoms, and my alcoholism, had pretty much wasted my value to U.S. employers, others, and to myself.

I discussed the job with Monica and we concluded that a fresh start, on a new continent, would be a great way to start over with a clean slate. I interviewed for the position offered and it seemed to go well. They told me that the likelihood that I would get the job was great, but the Australian business they were servicing would make the final decision. I would have to interview for the job at their headquarters, in Australia.

Perhaps if I run to another continent, my "memories" will fade and I might reclaim my former self.

Monica and I quickly wed in a civil ceremony in early 1974. We then obtained passports as husband and wife. The Australian Embassy accepted us as permanent immigrants. I booked a one-way passage for the two of us on a cruise ship, bound for Sydney, Australia.

Goodbye, America! You have done enough to me for two lifetimes!

Off we sailed. The ship was registered in Britain, but this was her final overseas voyage. She would spend the rest of her days sailing the seas around Australia and New Zealand.

Since most of the passengers were not American, being "Yankees" set us apart from them and the ship's crew. They took great amusement at our accent. They were mostly British, Australian, and New Zealanders. We took second seating for all our shipboard meals, dining at the Captain's Table. It was a jolly good time! We sailed for twenty days.

I received a shipboard telegram from Australian Mutual Provident (AMP), the target company about a week before we ported in Sydney. They had arranged an interview for me shortly after our arrival.

After we disembarked, we took an apartment close to the city and readied ourselves for a new life and, hopefully, new job. I was hired on the spot with the consulting firm and started work the following Monday.

I had a great position with the company. The first few months were filled with explorations of the neighborhood, marketplaces and shops. We also had to adapt to the lifestyle we found there. They drove on the left side of the street. Instead of learning how to do that safely, we chose not to buy a car. Shopping for groceries involved a couple of changes:

There were just a few supermarkets, which closed their businesses at 5:30 pm every day but Thursday. This meant once-a-week shopping along with a great majority of Sydney residents.

Standing in "queues" to hail a taxicab, carrying our purchases in our personal bags. The stores did not provide shopping bags, as they do in America.

This led to one of many adjustments we had to make. Monica had been married three times before she married me. She became pregnant shortly after we settled in.

In the year we lived there, the cost of living rose twenty-three percent. My salary rose a mere fifteen percent.

Australia had been a partner in the Vietnam War since the beginning, so in a sense the war followed us there. From 1974-75, Australia played only a humanitarian role in the conflict. On April 17th, 1975 Phnom Penh in Cambodia fell to the Khmer Rouge. Eight days later, Australia closed their embassy and began its own personnel airlift as Saigon's hold grew ever more tenuous. On April 30th, 1975 Communist forces captured Saigon as the last Americans left in now legendary scenes of panic and confusion[15].

I stopped paying Kathy the child support I owed her and the kids. Of course, this move to another job, in another land, was a failed attempt to run away from myself, and my demons.

---

[15] Vietnam Veterans Association of Australia, "A Chronology of Australian Involvement in Vietnam." (http://www.vvaa.org.au/calendar.htm)

Monica and I both yearned to return home. Our son Luke was born in September 1975 and we were on an airplane with one-way tickets bound for the United States just twenty-two days later. Our latest attempt to escape had lasted barely more than a year.

My attempt to become "somebody new" had failed.

Our interim destination was Tucson, Arizona. My parents, my sister and her family all lived a few miles from one another there. My folks had moved from Pasadena to Tucson while we were in Australia. We stayed with my sister for two weeks, getting adjusted to the time zone differences, and to being in America again.

My first trip to a supermarket was very impacting. I cried as I walked down the aisles, staring in wonderment at the plethora of canned and packaged goods. I now understood that we lived in a bountiful and prosperous country, and I have not deviated from that appreciation since my return from "down under."

I needed a job. We were nearly broke and had to get money, somehow.

I contacted a recruiter in Los Angeles and told him I was available for any kind of work he could find me. He worked with a data processing consultancy in Marina Del Rey, California. It was a joint venture wherein he would share a portion of his placement fees with the co-owner, and the co-owner would share the consulting services revenues with him.

The consulting side of the business had received a contract to do the systems analysis portion of an Inventory system, and the client needed someone who could start right away. I qualified for the assignment and was given the temporary job.

It took me a month to develop a system for their client, who was very appreciative for the work I had done. My next "gig" was with the 20th Century-Fox movie company, in Hollywood, who needed a temporary programmer for their General Ledger system while they looked for a full-time employee to take the spot. I was assigned to work there for a six-month contract.

While there, the consulting company courted me to work for them fulltime, rather than take the job at Fox. At the end of the contract, Fox offered me the job, but I declined. Instead, I worked on a variety of programming projects with the consulting company.

I liked not being an employee of any particular company. As a "consultant," I was able to quit jobs when I didn't like to do what they asked of me, and my resumé masked my poor coping skills. It read: "From (month, year) to (month, year) Consultant to various clients."

Predictably, one of the partners in the firm disliked my attitude. Psychologically, I was to a point where *whenever* I was told to do *anything* I disagreed with, I would challenge the deed. The partner insisted I do as I was told, and I told him he could take the project and put it up his own backside. I quit.

I was spiraling down, physically and emotionally, faster and faster with each passing day.

In 1977, I landed a job at Telecredit, a check guarantee corporation. Soon after I joined, a manager abruptly left the company; whether he was fired, or quit, I never knew. I was promoted and managed a group of twenty-some programmers and analysts.

This was a good job for me. Figuratively speaking, I was my boss. I even made a few friends. Unfortunately, a senior-management change occurred a year later. Senior management took direct control over the department. I was no longer my own boss and I was angry. I hated change. I reflected upon our Battalion's abrupt move to Da Nang. I remembered how upset that made me feel, and the same emotion was now filling my subconscious mind. Rather than accept the reorganization, I quit.

An owner-operator of hospitals around the nation hired me. There were a number of consultants working at this company and I began systematically replacing them with fulltime employees as fast as I could get away with. In a way, a strange way, I looked at them as ARVN (Army of the Republic of South Vietnam), and wanted my own men. The ARVN had been ineffectual, disorganized, and I thought contributed little to the overall effort. In my minds eye, it was like I was killing them off one at a time.

Of course, replacing the consultants drew the attention of the owner of the consulting services company. He invited me to visit his corporate offices in San Francisco, California on several occasions. I eventually accepted an invitation.

Toward the end of my trip, the owner offered me a job as Director of Projects. The pay was substantially more than I earned and the description of my duties sounded attractive. I accepted, and went to work for them in their Southern California branch office in 1978.

In 1979, I was transferred to the San Francisco branch office. It was a temporary reassignment. Monica stayed home in Southern California. I was given a corporate apartment in Sausalito, and a generous expense account. I did return frequently to L.A. to visit my family.

Within six months of transferring to San Francisco, my second marriage blew apart. We had created a second child together, a pretty girl we named Carissa.

I flew from the San Francisco Airport to Los Angeles and then up to Santa Barbara every Friday afternoon, and then reversed my travel the following Sunday nights. Monica would meet the plane and drive me to our home in Ventura.

What began as "big kiss" welcomes gradually weakened to short hugs when I stepped off the propeller-driven airplane. Later, the hugs went away and the drive home was a silent one.

The owner of the business offered to promote me to Vice President, with the condition that I relocate permanently to the Bay Area. There was to be a generous salary increase attached to the promotion. I discussed the proposition with Monica on my last trip back home. Monica flatly refused to relocate to San Francisco and, instead, told me that if I chose to accept the promotion she and I would divorce.

I would pay another price for "separating" from a close relationship. I felt I had no choice but to accept the job offer. There were no more weekend trips to Southern California. At least, the company would no longer pay the tab for the airline tickets, and my rise in pay wasn't enough for me to be able to afford the trips on my own.

I didn't miss my former wife, but the heartache of losing two more children was another blow to my fragile, low self-esteem. I regarded myself as a failure at being a husband and father.

Vivian, a saleswoman for Sony office equipment, entered my life one fortunate day. She was a young, attractive, single gal who wanted to sell her wares to our company. She offered to let us try the equipment for a week, free, so that we would see the benefits of using her Sony products.

I used the "free trial" opportunity to get to know her on a personal level. I didn't buy her products after the weeklong experiment, but I did ask her out on a date. The dates we went on blossomed into a romantic relationship and we began living together. She was fifteen years my junior. Our affair was doomed from the start, but my emotional instability denied me the clarity to perceive the impracticality of our cohabitation. The fact that I was much older than Vivian made our relationship vulnerable to the challenges that younger men would make to destroy it.

We bought a condominium in Foster City, near the San Francisco airport and established a home setting for ourselves.

By late 1982, I had managed to save seven thousand dollars (worth about $25,000 in today's currency, due to inflation). The owner of the company asked me to lend him six thousand dollars and said he'd pay me back twelve thousand within ninety days.

I lent him the money. He immediately became an absent business owner. Six months later I went to his San Francisco apartment to demand my money. This was extremely difficult to do. I didn't have the courage to stand up for my own rights. I found the courage, out of financial desperation, to confront him.

He told me that he was gay, that he'd blown the money on cocaine, and that I would have to get it out of the company. Eighteen months passed by before unpaid commissions equaled the original six grand. I had him sign a corporate check, payable to me, and I quit my job.

I had left the data processing community four years ago for that consulting services management job and I found that my skills were woefully out of date in 1983.

I had been out of the service for thirteen years when I learned there was going to be a Vietnam Veterans Memorial erected in the Washington, D. C. It was completed just two years later in November 1983.

My heart palpitated for a few seconds. *Well, better late than never!*

The fluttering only lasted a minute. Then came those pesky tears. Back then, my uncontrollable emotional flooding hit me whenever it felt like it. My silent teardrops streaked down my cheeks and were dripping onto my shirt collar, my breathing was shallow and labored, and my hands trembled so much I had to put down anything I was holding at the time.

As I saw it, my only employment opportunities were as a recruiter, salesman, or consulting services business owner. I had little money in the bank and couldn't afford to take time off for current programming classes.

In the years from 1984 to 1988 I had eighteen different jobs, and three half-year periods of unemployment. My alcohol abuse continued to escalate and had affected my work ethics. I was owed thousands of dollars in unpaid commissions, and my lover, Vivian, deserted me in 1986. A co-worker of hers, a man her age, courted Vivian away from me.

My mind was under a continuous barrage of recollections. I didn't connect with any one I worked with, and the work I did was under par for the abilities I once had. Some reasons I changed jobs was related to embarrassment of my performance, other reasons were my inability to interact with others, and other reasons were my inability to concentrate on a specific function for more than a few minutes. In short, I was a failure and failing miserably to perform.

That was it! I was certain I was going to have a nervous breakdown.

My personal debts had been accelerating at a pace far faster than my ability to gain employment, retain it, and pay the bills that relentlessly infected my mailbox day after day. I didn't know what to do. The rent on my apartment was due at the end of the month, as usual, and the first week of that month I had less than $3,000 left in my checking account. Of course I had no savings account to fall back on.

By chance, purely by chance, a former co-worker and I were talking on the phone about who was hiring, who was firing, and where we could look for work. He was out of a job, too.

"I know what we should do. At least I'm going to do it, as a last-ditch measure. You should consider doing it to." Wayne was always blunt and to the point.

"What should *we* do?"

"Declare bankruptcy. The lawyers handle all the paperwork, you get to keep the credit cards you plan to keep current, like American Express, and the rest of what you owe goes in the toilet. You are debt-free, my man!"

I told Wayne I'd have to think about it. "Stay by your phone for a few minutes. I'll call you back." I hung up the phone, poured a Gin over the remaining slivers of ice from my last drink, and sat on the couch, lights out.

Wayne's right. There is no other foreseeable option for either of us.

I finished my drink and called him back. We arranged to meet at his lawyer's office the next day. I was embarrassed, ashamed and felt like a dirt-bag, but I told the attorney that I wanted him to file the paperwork for me and be done with it. He did.

I kept the whole affair a secret until now, but since I am coming clean on the rest of my life in this memoir, I feel I owe it to you, dear reader, to know the "whole truth, and nothing but the truth." I have excellent credit today and plan on keeping it that way.

I needed to get help, but I didn't know where to turn. I called a Veterans' Service Officer nearby my office in Foster City, California and went in for a talk (I'll call him Joe). Over the phone, I told him I felt betrayed. I couldn't find another word to describe my anguish.

Joe said he worked with the Post-Traumatic Stress Disorder (PTSD) group at the VA, so I had hope. I talked to him for about an hour and a half. He was polite and a good listener. At the end of our session, he thanked me for coming in and showed me the door. That was the sum and substance of our visit.

I had not approached the VA for help, mostly because I was ashamed of my own attempts to overcome my emotional turmoil, and self-denial that I had any problems whatsoever. The VA might have offered alcohol dependency treatment, but they didn't know anything about me, and I never sought out help from them.

There was no relief or support offered or given. In fact, I was more upset when I left that meeting than when I'd arrived. So, being the brave U.S. Marine Corps combat veteran I was, I sent him a letter and said I wasn't coming back. Of course, I sent Joe a letter to avoid ever having to speak to him.

I picked up my problems and tried to cope with them as best I could.

About three months later Joe called me up and said, "We're going to have a Thursday evening group meeting at the VA in Menlo Park. I'm sure you'll get a lot out of it because it's all combat-experienced Vietnam vets and we know you're one. What do you think?"

"Sure. I'd be happy to." I thought I'd make some new friends. I didn't have many friends, especially vets.

The group of eleven, which met every week for two hours, with therapists Joe and Diane, was supposed to be for combat veterans. It turned out that only three of us had combat experience.

I stayed, much to my chagrin. I endured a year and some months of Thursday meetings, and being upset afterwards. As an example of the quality of help I received, the following incident occurred very shortly before I quit going there.

Two of the men in the group one evening had been in a minor disagreement at the beginning. Jeremy was combat-experienced. He wanted to keep things centered on Vietnam issues and situations: "This is when I was shot at," or "This is when I saw my best friend blown up. Let's keep it focused on Vietnam."

Wayne, who was not combat-experienced, wanted to deal with present-time issues: "I'm upset about something that happened today. I'm about to lose my job, my car is running rough, and I need new tires."

The therapists tried to defuse the situation. Whenever something was going awry in the group, they'd frequently call on me and "punch one of my buttons."

"David, tell us about one of your bad days. Please."

I would talk about some traumatic incident from my 'Nam days. I could easily talk for about forty-five minutes. That would run out the clock for the time they allotted for our sessions, and then they could send everybody home.

I told the group how upsetting and difficult that was to face my tour in today's setting. I said that the pictures that came up from those seven months in early 1967 send me reeling. That night I related my R&R experiences to the group, which included the utter dread I felt the whole time I was flying back to 'Nam. I cried a long time toward the end of my talk.

After I dried up my tears, Joe, with no regard for me or my current mental state, nor a "thank you," nor any other acknowledgment, turned to the group and said "Well, we're just about out of time now, but before we break up I want to make sure that the disagreement we had earlier tonight doesn't affect the group. We're all going to be here next week, aren't we?"

That was a Thursday night. The group adjourned. There was simply silence, indicating a lack of disagreement or interest in an argument. There didn't seem to be any reason not to meet next Thursday.

I got in my car and headed back up the freeway to Foster City. I was unfit to drive, but I had no alternative. My rage was past the boiling point and I couldn't extinguish the flames in my mind.

I forgot I was driving. I was, mentally, sitting on my couch staring at the wall across from me and watching the "film" of my helicopter jump to stay with Jones and the others, instead of being a "coward" who left the scene of the battle.

I came half awake and saw that my car had drifted from the fast lane I had been in well over to the rightmost lane, about to strike the shoulder of the freeway. I slammed on my brakes, locked my arms at my elbows, and leaned my head slightly forward.

My groin constricted like it did when I jumped into an icy-cold swimming pool, my breathing stopped and my eyes bulged nearly out of their sockets. The grip I had on the steering wheel should have bent it, I was squeezing it so hard.

My car spun into a 360-degree circle in a distance of about a hundred meters, and then stalled just short of falling off the freeway. I looked around to see if I'd hit anyone or anything. I hadn't. I slapped my right cheek, hard, with my right palm, causing my ears to ring. I took a deep breath, then another, then another. I started up the car and drove home in the slow lane, vowing out loud that I would never let my mind wander, ever again, if I were behind the wheel. Later, I would eventually give my car away, no longer trusting myself to drive.

I went home, turned off the lights, mentally got back on that airplane going from Hawaii to Vietnam and got off that plane on Sunday night. I was returning to 'Nam, and my certain death.

I didn't leave my apartment to eat, buy cigarettes or do anything else. And of course I spoke to no one during that time.

I had kept my traumatic experiences to myself for years and years, and for good reasons, in my opinion. The early years were "dangerous" ones for returning combat-experienced servicemen. I exerted much of my mental strength to keep my military background out of the public light.

With no one, nor any agency to turn to for help with my traumas, I stuffed them inside my mind. There they festered and grew more severe. My soul, I felt, had been lacerated many times over and my wounds didn't heal.

I assumed I was opening up my Pandora's Box at the right place, the VA, and to the right therapists, in the safe companionship of like-suffering comrades. My assumptions were all invalidated; the VA didn't have the tools to help me, the therapists enhanced their respective résumés, rather than treat the likes of me, and the majority of comrades were not combat-experienced.

11 Traumatic Incident Reduction

The only good thing that did come out of those meetings was that I met Pieter there, a handsome, friendly South-African. He was a man who struggled to fight off the effects of PTSD with drugs to no avail. Pieter tried to get help from the VA. That didn't work, either. His recovery came about through TIR sessions. In a 1990 interview with Bob Moore, PhD, Pieter said:

> On January 13th, 1987 I was a heroin addict out of control in Phoenix, AZ. I finally became suicidal and was taken in by a fellow Vietnam vet who insisted I come with him. He knew what I was going to do and took me to the VA hospital in Menlo Park, California. I was in the hospital for a year; I ended up in a psychiatric unit for PTSD.

> Since being released from the VA hospital, I went to work with Dr. Gerbode and with Gerald French. They have a technique which is called Traumatic Incident Reduction (TIR). It is not psychology and it's not psychotherapy, in fact what it really is is an educational procedure. The root of the word education has at its root "drawing out". You draw out what a person already knows.

> In this procedure, you become aware of exactly what it is that is troubling you and you get to take a new look at what decisions you made or what you did not get complete looking at. It is non-evaluative and nobody is going to tell you that you are good or bad. Having somebody else tell you why you did it, how you felt, the reasons you're doing what you're doing, is absolutely ridiculous.

> Unlike what happened to me before, once I had done this I no longer have a problem with these incidents affecting me in my present life. What we've found so far is that after 15 to 40 hours of TIR, the PTSD symptoms are gone.

Pieter and I became fast friends. We were both combat-experienced. We shared a sixth-sense affinity that went beyond friendship. Through Pieter, I met Gerald French, a Santa Claus looking-type, who was a facilitator at The Institute for Research of Metapsychology (IRM). The IRM was located in a small nondescript office building. It had a couple of business offices, and rooms where classes were taught, like Communication, and private rooms where TIR was practiced.

In 1998, the IRM would later transform into the worldwide association of professionals now known as the Traumatic Incident Reduction Association or TIRA (info at www.TIR.org).

I talked to Pieter and Gerald. I told them I was interested in what they had done, because it sounded a lot better than what I had received at the VA.

Gerald said, "Hey, have a look at the Effective Communication course the Institute offers."

Pieter and I took the course together. What I got out of it was an ability to communicate how I felt in a more controlled manner. I subsequently applied the skills I learned in all my communications, verbal and written.

I learned that the Institute offered facilitation. Pieter had done what was called *viewing* with Gerald and had tremendous success. I expressed an interest in that as well. I hoped I could get some help with my PTSD problems. Gerald let me know that there might be a chance that he could work with me. The process is called Traumatic Incident Reduction (TIR).

I leapt at the chance. There were lots of events that I "stuffed." Stuffing meant I repressed traumatic experiences. They were still in my mind and would not go away on their own. Stuffing *did not* work! There were numerous occasions when my memories were re-stimulated.

I would have unsolicited recollections of traumatic episodes I had experienced in 'Nam. They were not memories. Instead, the experiences were like my having been teleported back into my horrific past, where I would see, hear, smell, feel, and touch the environment I was taken back to, to relive it in real-time, here and now.

A recap of my traumatic episodes follows. These were most of my thoughts that randomly assaulted my days (flashbacks) and nights (nightmares). Each experience is listed below and followed by my mislabeling of it. I hope this illustrates the repressions which I found so hard to manage.

- *Froze with fright, standing up, the first time I was under fire.*

  I had labeled this as performance anxiety.

- *Watched two marines try to break open the skull of a dead Viet Cong with a large rock.*

  This label was about underperformance, and I felt that this kind of behavior would be replicated on me if I failed at a task or assignment.

- *Observed a marine intentionally shoot a girl four or six years of age.*

  This manifested itself as a fear of being fired "on the spot."

- *Watched the girl's grandfather carry the girl into our line of fire, sobbing.*

  The thought that no one would come to my aid in my time of need left me feeling empty and alone.

- *Had a lieutenant who delighted in sneaking up on me when I was on watch at night.*

  I was forever "watching my back," in case any one tried to harm me.

- *Was offered a blood-soaked flak jacket and a helmet with a bullet hole through it as part of my first field equipment.*

  Sure, I could get hired at a new company, but they gave me the worst jobs, with the lowest income yield.

- *Had my boots rot off during an operation in the field.*

  I was compulsively groomed, well-dressed, and polished, head to foot.

- *Rifle-butted a girl of twelve in the face when she would not move away.*

  Suppressed rage when subordinates wouldn't "Just do what I told you to do."

- *Discovered brain matter on barbed wire I was stretching out.*

  I abhorred doing what I was told to do, regardless of my attitude about the task.

- *Observed a marine laugh as he stepped on the chest of a dead Viet Cong and watched blood squirt out of the enemy's wounds.*

  When I made a mistake, others took pleasure at my failings.

- *Awoke to find a buffalo leech on my leg.*

  Cleanliness was first and foremost, above all else.

- *Was abandoned under fire when a rocket jammed in my launcher.*

  I was on my own, regardless if I needed help from others.

- *Was abandoned under fire when I was shot.*

  I'm all by myself, and there was no one I could count on for help.

- *Hit head in open field. Watched my fellow marines run by me to seek cover for themselves (abandonment).*

  Don't make a mistake because it could cost me my livelihood.

- *Received letters from wife telling me how much fun she and a girlfriend had on weekend nights when they went out to bars to dance and drink.*

  I'm fine and having fun, you suffer and just "take it."

- *Watched fellow marine shoot himself in the foot to get evacuated.*

  I can "take it" on the job, no matter how much I want out of here.

- *Heard same man cry in his sleep when he was returned to duty.*

  The futility of trying to "tough it out" regardless of the measures I took to make things better for myself.

- *Found marine boot with foot in it in a hedgerow.*

  Watch out for any surprises. They will gross me out.

- *Saw Lt. Spivey hit a head-height booby trap.*

  God gets even. Bad behavior brings on enormous repercussions.

- *Nearly murdered villager for stealing my laundry.*

  Anger management gone awry. My need to control my rage outbursts.

- *Watched Prestridge testing his new M-16 by shooting a woman getting water from a nearby well.*

  Callous disregard for the harm I could inflict on others.

- *Identified Haas's remains.*

  An aversion to attending anyone's funeral.

- *Exchanged letters with Haas's mother.*

  A desire to please others who suffer the experiences of trauma.

- *Had an artillery canister fall six inches in front of my head.*

  Fear of any unforeseen noises.

- *Bullets sounding like bees digging up ground all around me.*

  There are no safe places, and no safe times.

- *Nearly trapped in Da Nang village my last night in Vietnam.*

  Fear of being unarmed, or inexperienced for the job at hand.

- *Robbed by marines while I slept in Okinawa after tour was over.*

  Trust no one, at any time, regardless of how well you know them.

- *Circled over El Toro base for two hours so that President Johnson could land and be photographed greeting returning veterans.*

  The "real heroes" are the ones that can take the glory, just by their hierarchy position.

My combat experiences traveled a troubled path in my mind. When I first came home, the images were vivid and lay in my conscious memory bank. Since they were so graphic, and since no one asked about them (nor cared), I suppressed them. I forbade myself to recall them or go through them again.

My alcohol abuse escalated dramatically. I *do* take credit for holding firm on my resolve not to drink until the day's work was done. Without anyone or any agency to turn to, I chose to drink at night until I lost consciousness. Then, I had convinced myself, I could sleep without nightmares. The nightmares remained, but I was so drunk I fell back to sleep without remembering their contents.

As time went on, my *suppression* of such thoughts became a *repression* of them. I incorrectly re-labeled them, attaching new relationships of them with everyday circumstances. For instance, punctuality was very important to me. If I was late for an appointment, or someone was late for an appointment with me, I would become unduly upset.

Cleanliness and tidiness of my surroundings and me were obsessions; everything had to be meticulously preserved.

I made very, very few friends, and my female relationships were over-brimming with fears of separation and loss.

Superiors in my workplace were cruel and harsh, and I didn't trust any of them.

Confrontation with others was simply out of the question. I sought *any other way* to resolve conflicts of this nature. Later, you will read about my TIR session, which forever after resolved this nightmarish condition of mine.

TIR work succeeded in recovering my experiences, resolved the pain associated with them, gave them clarity, correctly labeled them, and ultimately allowed me to experience them as mere memories.

For a great deal of time I thought of myself as a mailman, sorting my memories as I would letters, to be filed in their correct mail box and then moving on to the next "letter." My traumatic experiences had no "address" and so fell on the filing room floor, again and again. They would float up time after time, seeking a delivery slot where they could reside. There was *never* a place to put them away, and to rest.

I worked with Gerald as my Facilitator for approximately twenty hours over the course of three weeks: I began sleeping through most nights, something I hadn't been able to do before I received quality help.

My alcohol consumption gradually tapered off. I became a "social" drinker.

I could now remember some of my dreams.

I've had other private victories too.

For example, I couldn't sing the "Star Spangled Banner" from start to finish without tearing up and choking on the words. Though I haven't tried, I'm sure I could get through the first stanza.

All my "wins" were a direct outcome of my work with Traumatic Incident Reduction. I feel that TIR, as its practiced by a trained facilitator, works for PTSD casualties and it applies to any group of troubled, less able people, whether their PTSD is combat-related or not.

This was TIR, as I knew it then, where it was conducted, how it was conducted with me, and my outcome of one session. Today you can find TIR practiced in many places around the world, from Alaska to Brazil and from Australia to Russia.

My recollection of my first experience with TIR follows.

The room was small. It was about the size of a standard business cubicle, except it had four sides, an overhead ceiling light that provided a dim light, and it had a door, which was closed.

A small desk was centered in the room (where the facilitator would take brief notes). Two chairs, with armrests, sat facing each other on opposite sides of the desk.

This is where I sat one evening in 1988, alone with my thoughts, waiting for the arrival of Gerald. I was forty-seven years old. I was breathing heavily and softly crying. Prior to this session, I had undergone a detailed intake interview highlighting the nature of my symptoms and unwanted feelings that I wished to release.

It was 7:20 pm and the Northern California night sky was just dark enough to allow a view of some stars. The temperature was typical of the Bay Area, balmy and comfortable. I had finished my usual evening meal, consisting of a meat-and-potatoes TV dinner, and I knew I would have room for a good fifth of gin after I got home.

My session with Gerald was to begin at 7:30 pm, and, as I always strived to do, I was early. I was cynical, yet brave. Whatever Gerald threw at me, I was more than ready to face it, and prevail. I was unfamiliar with the TIR procedure. God knows, I had my share of traumatic experiences, but the concept of "reducing" a trauma was foreign and, seemingly, impossible for me to comprehend.

Gerald entered the room, shook hands with me, and took the chair opposite mine. He smiled and asked me to make myself comfortable. Although our session was performed with biomonitoring, most practitioners today just work face-to-face without any instrumentation.

The session lasted exactly as long as it needed to. We took no breaks, as it was slowly restoring my energy rather than fatiguing me. We stayed focused on the one theme I had presented to him, and no other: my difficulty with confronting people. The work that I did at times seemed like manual labor, though I never left the chair I sat in.

Time was irrelevant, it seemed, because neither Gerald nor I had anywhere else to be at that time; just where we were, talking about just what we were talking about.

After the TIR experience, my mood was jovial and my lungs felt like they had just breathed my first quart of oxygen in over twenty years. I was laughing and smiling, and it was not acting; I was genuinely happy. I had not felt this emotion for many, many years. I went home, ignored the gin I had planned to drink, and peacefully fell asleep (in my bed, no less!)

After spending time with Gerald, working the TIR routine, I was fortunate to meet another fine gentleman. Tom Joyce had attended the third annual IRM Conference in 1989, where I was honored to give a speech about some of my Vietnam and TIR experiences.

Tom is a cordial man. He is very smart, and handsome. Tom introduced himself to me and we chatted briefly. He told me he was a freelance writer and that he liked my speech. Tom asked me if he could interview me for an article he was currently working on and I agreed, enthusiastically.

Tom captured every aspect of my TIR session in his groundbreaking article "Back Into The Heart of Darkness"[16]. It voices the experience I had with Gerald that first session. What follows is a brief excerpt from that article.

---

[16] The complete text can be found in *Beyond Trauma: Conversations on Traumatic Incident Reduction, 2nd Ed.*, 2005, Loving Healing Press.

David stares down at the table. His eyes are narrowed and his face ruddy, like a man who is exerting an enormous amount of effort to escape from something dark and terrifying that breeds in the murky outback of his mind.

"Have another look," says the man with a silver beard, sitting opposite David. He is big and benign, his features almost elfin, he brings all his presence into the communication yet remains unobtrusive.

David recounts the story for the third time and there is a perceptible edge to his voice, as if his boredom is curdling into frustration. "The District Manager and I had this verbal agreement concerning the percentage of sales I would receive. But he decided to rearrange the commission structure before I was paid. We're talking about nearly seven thousand dollars here. Damn it, I earned that money."

David breathes deeply and closes his eyes. His square jaw clenches tightly, and when he continues, there is a slight trembling in his voice. "I know that I have to confront him. But every time I even think about doing it, my stomach just knots up."

David's face flushes with the pigment of rage and humiliation. "Here I am, this bad-ass former U.S. Marine, black belt martial artist, scared (to death) over the thought of demanding money that's owed me. I don't know why people always take advantage of me. I don't know why I let them."

David stops and swallows hard. He looks up, angst radiating from icy blue eyes, and shrugs resignedly, signifying that he's once again reached "the wall"—a barrier beyond which he cannot penetrate.

The bearded man nods in genuine empathy. "Okay," he acknowledges. "Now, take a look and tell me if there is an earlier, similar incident."

David pulls a deep breath into his lungs, closes his eyes and attempts to pierce that tenebrous cloud of the past, where unspeakable phantasms lurk and disturb the sanctity of sleep.

"Yeah, there," he says, "what do you see right there?"

Suddenly, David is a 25-year old Lance Corporal, walking through the bush near Chu Lai. It is December of 1966, and he is on his ninety-second patrol in Vietnam. There is the smell of rain-soaked foliage and warm, redolent earth. It is dusk and the mosquitoes are beginning to swarm at the smell of human sweat. There are the sounds of jungle life signaling the ingress of night and, above them all, there is the sound of his own heart pumping adrenaline into his veins. It is not like a recollection, some vague distant memory. He is there, in the grip of saline fear, which has possessed him from the moment his boots touched Vietnamese soil. He has nearly eleven more months of this hell to live through before they will lift his feet out of that fetid green nightmare.

When the sniper fire begins, David is hit in the chest by AK-47 fire. He rolls onto one knee and wields his 3.5 rocket launcher, instinctively aiming toward the outcropping of trees he believes to be the enemy position. He calls for his A-Gunner to stand by for loading, but the eighteen-year-old balks and runs for the nearest cover. David, fuming with anger, rises up. Pain excoriates reason; no emotion survives but rage.

As soon as David can reach the tree line he fully intends to beat the living hell out of the callow grunt that left him with his life on the line.

It is all in slow motion now, the loping run toward the trees, the sound of "popcorn" and the rush of wind as bullets rip past his ears. There is the blood drenching his flack jacket, the numbing in his chest and the overwhelming anger rising in him with the pressure of an erupting geyser.

And now he spots the A-Gunner, a solid gray silhouetted against the variegated gray of the bush, barely human in appearance, his hands shaking with a spastic intensity of fear. And in those hands is an M14 automatic assault rifle, safety thrown, aimed directly at David's chest.

David exhales an expletive, and only then realizes he's been holding his breath a good fifteen seconds. "Christ! I just backed off, real easy. 'It's only a flesh wound, man. No problem.' I knew if I even looked cross-eyed at this kid he would blow me away."

The bearded man nods, signifying understanding. "I got that," he says. David knows he has. "Go to the start of the incident and tell me when you've done so."

David does so, three more times. At first it is painful, then boring, and then, on the fourth recounting, David chuckles to himself. It is a small escape of air, which accompanies a great explosion of clarity.

The bearded man nods and queries, "How are you doing?"

David looks up and his eyes sparkle with amusement. "I'm doing fine."

His face has relaxed as if some emotional pillory has been lifted from his neck. "It's a stupid thing, really. It just occurred to me that not all the people I have to confront in life are armed and dangerous. I guess it's safe to be upset if you've got a good reason to be."

The bearded man returns David's broad smile; it's hard to judge which of them feels a greater sense of accomplishment at this moment. "Thanks. We'll end right here."

Gerald and I addressed most of my major problems. The resulting improvements allowed me to enter the work force again with renewed strength and a much-improved view of my fellow man.

The traumatic incidents that we worked through in TIR removed the "charge" that they had had, and the emotional devastation I would chronically go through as a result. As a side effect, some of the less-charged traumas seemed to diminish as a result of "handling" the Big Ones.

After my Traumatic Incident Reduction work, with Gerald as my facilitator, my countenance shifted dramatically. The edge of my personality, my hyper-vigilant state, changed from being like the sharp edge of a sword into something more akin to a smooth automobile bumper. Calmness fell over me for the first time in decades.

12   Recovery

Perhaps, I thought, not all people are predisposed to do me harm. My self-image improved; I was no longer emotionally frail. I knew that my next employment environment would seem less threatening and I would be more productive than I had previously been.

I approached a former consulting services competitor of mine and asked the benevolent owners, a husband and wife team, if they could use my services. I was pleased to receive two positions to choose from. I decided to work as a sales consultant, instead of as a recruiter. I sold the condominium in Foster City and took an apartment in San Francisco.

I was feeling productive, had a few successes, and was getting along quite well with the other employees. TIR had done me no harm and had significantly altered my perception of what it was like to be a productive citizen in the marketplace.

I retained my friendship with Pieter, but our face-to-face visits grew less and less frequent.

Pieter suggested that I file a claim for compensation with the Veterans Administration (VA), basing my claim on the fact that I was a PTSD casualty. He had encouraged me to do that several times before, but I rejected the notion on the basis that I was not damaged at all.

This time I took his encouragement to heart. I did so because of the valuable, priceless insights I achieved while working with TIR. After having suffered nearly two decades of PTSD at this point, I felt that compensation would be the ultimate acknowledgment of my unsung service and suffering.

The VA had a downtown office within walking distance from my San Francisco employer, so on one of my lunch breaks I went in and got the claim forms I would have to fill out. The main body of the claim consisted of recounting, in graphic detail, the traumatic incidents I thought resulted in the development of PTSD.

It was still somewhat emotionally troubling to me as I wrote my claim. However, I found that if I applied my new Effective Communication tools to the task, I was able to give a third-party account of what happened.

I regained my composure within a few hours of completing my claim. Before TIR, such a revisiting of my past would have ended in a bout of self-medication and hiding out in my apartment for a few days.

After submitting my claim, I went back to work and put the matter into the far recesses of my mind. Weeks passed before I heard from the VA. It was good news, in that they did not summarily dismiss my statements. They scheduled a psychiatric evaluation for me at the VA Medical Center in town.

The interview lasted less than half an hour. It was not as probative or as challenging as I thought it was going to be. The doctor was a few years younger than I, and I felt that he had an appreciation for my condition, and a modicum of respect for what I tried to do for my comrades and my country. After the interview, we shook hands and parted company.

Another period of time elapsed before I heard from the VA. This time it was the announcement that my PTSD symptoms had been rated at thirty-percent disabled. I was going to receive a small monetary monthly compensation, psychological counseling, and was now eligible for Vocational Rehabilitation, which could include up to four years of college education.

The money was nice, just under two hundred dollars per month. I thought maybe I could get involved with Voc Rehab at some future date. The rewarding feeling of having my emotional scars validated made my whole experience valid.

I went on about the business of "being the new me" with a renewed spirit. I continued to do well until the United States went to war with Iraq in January 1991, calling the conflict "Desert Storm." The start of Desert Storm brought out feelings and memories I had locked away for almost a quarter of a century.

When I had returned from combat, I was twenty-six years old. I was released from active duty in April 1968. Back then; the mood of the country was very disapproving of the whole Viet Nam situation. Angry mobs marched through the streets, shouting their disdain for the war, and the warrior (I thought). This new resentment of servicemen and their mission greatly bothered me.

At that time, I was living in a San Francisco, California apartment, five floors up from the street, with a balcony. The balcony looked straight down over a street named "Battery Street." It is one of the main streets in the Financial District.

One evening soon after the war started, I heard loud noises coming from below. I stepped out onto my balcony and looked down. Below me, I observed a mob of approximately a thousand young men and women, marching on the street.

They were shouting anti-war slogans, breaking windows of buildings and automobiles, turning over trash containers, and other bad behaviors. I became re-stimulated and the old fears I felt after my homecoming, and the subsequent years that followed, resurfaced.

However, my TIR work was paying me dividends, again. I was not the "returning vet" that evening; I knew it was 1991. My only fears that night were for my physical safety. I telephoned my sister and told her that I was worried what might happen to me.

Somewhere in the conversation, while she tried to extinguish my anxiety, I told her that I was going to start carrying a club underneath my suit jacket. We talked for about half an hour, and then I said my goodbyes.

An hour passed by. I had all my lights turned out and was sitting rigidly on my sofa. At about 10 pm the phone rang and when I answered it, it was my mother on the other end of the line.

She, and dad convinced me that for everyone's safety and sanity, I should leave San Francisco, move to live with them, temporarily, and take up residence in Tucson, Arizona.

It sounded like that's what I needed to do, so I gave notice at my job, packed what I wanted in the trunk of my car, sold my furniture, and drove straight through to their home.

Now I needed to form a plan of action.

I surveyed the data processing environment, but there were no consulting service businesses that I could identify with. I concluded that my programming skills were years behind my peers.

I settled into my parents' spare bedroom and had a separate telephone line installed. I had been there for about a month before I had a revelation. I needed to establish a "mental health paper trail."

I was eligible for VA Vocational Rehabilitation, and what better time to take advantage of those benefits than now?

I went to see the Service Officer in town and began another paperwork trail, seeking a college education, with a degree in Computer Science as my goal.

The "wheels" of Government moved swiftly in the state of Arizona. I was accepted into a college program, and given a work-study job at the VA Medical Center as a twenty-hour per week clerk. I enrolled at the local Junior College, taking classes that gave me thirteen credits a semester.

I found a furnished studio apartment and moved from my parents' home to there, about twenty minutes away from them. I also renewed a telephone friendship with another Marine, Terry, I had met in that infamous therapy group.

Terry was nineteen years old when a Viet Cong sniper shot him. The single bullet wound left him permanently disabled as an incomplete quadriplegic. He had been living in Menlo Park, California when he attended the "rap group" I was in.

Terry later moved back to his birthplace in Warwick, Rhode Island. He and I talked for weeks and weeks about what we were both doing with our time. One night, Terry asked me what my percentage of disability was.

"Thirty percent."

"You should appeal your claim."

How could it hurt me if I did that?

He also suggested that I file a Social Security (SS) disability claim at the same time. I didn't think that it would do much good, but I went ahead with my appeal and the Social Security claim.

One of the SS claim forms was a psychological evaluation sheet. My VA therapist filled it out for me. I heard from the Social Security Administration first.

They scheduled me for an interview with a doctor to evaluate my claim that I lacked the emotional stability to gain and hold fulltime employment, due to PTSD. It would take months before a decision would be made, so I just went back to my temporary job and student pursuits.

The government contacted me soon after the first interview I had with one of their doctors. They concluded that I was unemployable and acknowledged that I was one hundred percent disabled, and gave me over a thousand dollars a month for compensation.

At the same time the VA took note of my combat experiences, and the fact that I was in Voc Rehab. They raised my disability rating to fifty percent and told me they would re-examine my condition in about two years. I took the award letter to my VA Service Officer and asked him for his advice.

He told me to discontinue my Voc Rehab program "without prejudice" (so I could go back on it if Social Security changed their mind), quit the work-study job, and plan for my retirement, which was now at hand. At the end of the semester, I did those things.

I had to figure out what I was going to due with my time, being retired at the age of fifty-three.

I was retired with lots of idle time on my hands. I began cooking my own meals, instead of heating up frozen dinners, or going to restaurants and eating by myself in the middle of a large crowd.I looked for recipes that would challenge my mediocre kitchen skills. I would shop the grocery store daily, and then cook in the afternoon.

I became extremely bored of my own company. I joined a local Veterans of Foreign Wars Post as a lifetime member and began drinking beers and shooting billiards several nights a week. I enjoyed the pool games and the buzz that the beers gave me, but the membership sorely lacked Vietnam veteran members. This grew old and I stopped going after a year, or so.

The VA two-year review of my case came up. This review noted that I was on Social Security Disability, along with an examination of my daily habits and social life, or in my case, the lack of them.

What other factors they considered, I have no idea. The result was an increase to seventy percent, temporarily rated at one hundred percent because I could not hold a fulltime job. This was good news and resulted in more monthly monetary compensation.

In 1993, the news was making a big fuss about the 10th anniversary re-dedication of "The Wall" (The Memorial came to be known as just that). My buddy, Terry in Rhode Island, the man I'd met at the V.A. "Rap" group chided me over the phone to go see the Wall. "What better time to go than now. If you skip this opportunity you'll probably *never* go." I agreed with him. After we hung up, I arranged my travel plan to coincide with the Wall's anniversary, November 11th.

Suddenly, I found myself on a plane bound for Washington. I landed at 9:30 pm and checked into my hotel room before 11:00. I took off my suit, dress shirt, and tie, and then donned the Levis and sweatshirt I had in my suitcase. Down to the lobby I went, got walking directions to the Memorial from the night clerk, and headed straight for it.

As I approached the right side of the Wall, I felt calm and unemotional. I looked up the panel where Kenny Haas' name was inscribed. I started at one end of the Wall, moving at a slow, deliberate pace. My eyes scanned every name I passed without having read any of them, and found myself at Kenny's panel.

There was his name, just in front of me. I touched it with my right fingertip and traced each letter. There were no tears and I didn't tremble. I resumed my stroll and reached the other end. I took a few steps forward to the sidewalk, turned around for another look, then returned to my room for the night.

How weird! Why didn't I break down, fall to my knees and wail like a newborn baby? My mind refused to cough up an answer for me. I went to bed and to sleep.

My 7:00 am "wake up call" came right on time. I shaved, showered, dressed just like the night before and headed straight back to the Wall.

There were many, many more people gathered there than last night. We all participated in the re-dedication ceremony. After the fanfare, I walked straight to Kenny's panel, stood at attention, saluted his name, gave thanks to all the names inscribed there, and then cried.

The cry wasn't painful. I flashed on the reason for my behavior the night before, and now as I stood there weeping. TIR had cleared up my muddled recollection of Ken's death, and I could cry just like any other normal, emotional person!

God, what a relief!

I visited the Wall the next day, for a few minutes, and then caught a taxicab to the airport. I returned to California, drove home, smoked a cigarette in my darkened apartment, and then went to bed for another good night's sleep.

Things were going OK. Then, while visiting my mom one morning, I noticed a marked difference in her facial expression. I was certain that she had had a stroke. Half of her face seemed to have slipped downward. Her speech was a little garbled.

I told dad to make an appointment with her doctor right away. I took mom to the doctor's office and he confirmed my suspicion. We arranged to have her put under the care of a nurse in a specialized nursing home. Mom spent the night there, and dad and I returned home and waited for tomorrow to come so we could get a prognosis of mom's condition.

At around 10 am he and I went to see mom. They had done some preliminary assessments of her condition, the treatment she would need to undergo, and a probable date when she could come back home, about six weeks from now, if things went according to their expectations. Her therapy began that afternoon.

I visited her each day, in the late afternoon. Dad was usually there some time before me. Mom had some problems walking unassisted, but she was ambulatory. Her biggest obstacle to overcome was her speech and short-term memory. The speech pathologist was very strict with my mother, and mom grew increasingly frustrated with her, and the way the therapist treated her. In mom's opinion, she was bossy and thought that mom was just being stubborn with the exercises.

Mom wanted to be out of the nursing home at back at her house with dad as soon as possible. She was a very tenacious individual.

The evening before the morning that she was going to be released to home care, mom had to use the restroom. She decided she would walk there by herself, unassisted by hospital personnel. After all, she was being released and she was "just fine on her own."

The fall she sustained on the way back to her bed broke her pelvis. She was found on the floor an hour later when there was a shift change at the home. They rushed her, via ambulance, to the hospital where she underwent hip replacement surgery. I later had an opportunity to read the notes of her surgery, which mentioned stopped-heart episodes. They had to resuscitate her several times.

After a week of hospital confinement, she was returned to the specialized nursing home. Mom was in a vegetative state, going in and out of consciousness often. After four or five subsequent visits to her bedside I knew that I was not going to see my mother anymore. I felt like I was going to a funeral service for her each time I saw her. I told dad that I felt like I did at grandma's funeral and that I was not going to visit her again, unless she returned home.

Six weeks of waiting for a miracle was time poorly spent. She died while I was at a Disabled Veterans Ski Clinic in Colorado. I was taking some quality time off to see Terry and meet some of his colleagues. My sister, Susan telephoned the news to me as I sat at a dinner table with Terry and three other men.

After the call, I called the table to order and we toasted her ascent into God's hands. Susan and her husband took care of the cremation and all the other details for us.

Back home, dad was taking the loss of his wife very badly. He cried most days and just moped around the condominium they had shared. I was living alone and dad took to inviting me to come live with him. I did not want to hurt him, and at the same time I did not want to be around him as he mourned his loss and faced his lonely future. I had to repeatedly decline his requests, which placed a strain on our relationship.

I did accompany him on a weeklong vacation to La Jolla, California. It was the last place the two of them had vacationed in before we lost her.

We sat in the apartment every day, pretending to watch television. In reality, dad just sat and sobbed at the loss of his wife, and only friend.

The toll on his health was dramatic and sad to behold. He lost weight, began trembling so that he could barely sign the checks he wrote to pay the monthly bills. Though all of his immediate family sorely wanted him to pull out of it, we knew he was inconsolable.

Eventually, he checked himself into a hospice and quietly died. Susan and her husband took care of the cremation and all the other details for us.

The estate they left for Susan and me to share amounted to about fifty thousand dollars. Susan insisted that we divide it equally and I accepted. I thought it would be foolish to just put it into a savings account, so I began researching the stock market.

I chose the Edward Jones investment firm. I used the money to buy mutual funds and over the next few years, 1994 through 1996, the funds were turning a nice, modest profit. My daytime activities now included watching hours of CNN, which tracked the stock market on a minute-to-minute basis. I took my extra monthly income and began buying technology stocks on an individual basis. This also worked well for my growing estate. I really felt like I wanted to get a life for myself.

I had not wanted to have an intimate relationship since my breakup in 1987. I had always thought women were appealing, and that I would sometime have a mate to share my future with, but I knew that I was quite a package to put up with.

Funny, until 1996 I had not thought to find out if my TIR successes would translate into being able to become emotionally vulnerable. I told myself that I was going to put "David" into the singles environment and see what would happen.

I had more than enough dress-up suits, seven or eight of them, from my business days. They were custom tailored, so they were kind of ageless and still socially current. I had plenty of shirts and ties, as well.

I lived in an apartment complex that afforded me the luxury of walking from my apartment to a small shopping center and some other small businesses. There was an upscale restaurant in the mini-mall. It was across the hall from a real estate firm, who employed a number of women realtors.

I took advantage of the proximity of the restaurant/bar, to perhaps meet some potentially single, attractive women patrons I could approach.

My timing was not the greatest. I cunningly thought that Thursdays, Fridays, and Saturdays would be the best evenings to meet women. As it turned out, those were the best nights, but the clientele was mostly men. I shifted my attention to the menu, plying the recipes of some of the dishes they offered for dinner. Then I tried to replicate them in my humble kitchen. Some successes and some failures followed.

My casual conversations with the patrons felt comfortable and my confidence and self-esteem grew. I spent several months enjoying the ambiance of the bar, and the company of the acquaintances I met there.

One fine evening, after I had consumed a gin martini (or two), and filled with a sense of self-worth, a lovely woman came in with a realtor I had befriended. His name escapes me, but the woman was named Susan.

She was very attractive and, I thought, approachable. I dared myself to get off my familiar barstool and join her for light conversation. It took some internal "muscle" to get up, move over toward her, and ask if I could join her.

She said, "Expect nothing from me, but know that you are welcome to sit next to me, provided you are interesting and that you pay for my wine." I gladly accepted the agreement, and the terms, and took a stool next to her.

We talked and talked about everything under the sun. I tried to kiss her a couple of times, but only got the privilege of caressing her cheek. We exchanged telephone numbers and I walked her to her car, bidding a fond farewell. I walked home and had a wonderful night's sleep. Maybe something good would come of this chance encounter, I thought.

I married Susan a year later; we now have a miraculous relationship of the kind I had given up on ever finding.

About the Author

David W. Powell is a native Southern Californian. He was born in East Los Angeles in 1941, and lived in Long Beach, Pasadena, Arcadia, Redondo Beach, and Ventura until his relocation to Northern California in the early 1980's. There, he lived in Sausalito, Foster City, Palo Alto, and Downtown San Francisco. David migrated to Australia in 1974, and then returned to live in Southern California in 1975.

He has been married three times and is the father of four children, Jason, Carissa, Scott, and Thomas.

His vocation was in the computer environment. He was a first, second, and third generation computer programmer, systems analyst, project leader, manager, vice president, executive vice president, and owned his own computer consulting services company.

He graduated from high school and attended several semesters of college courses.

He was a first generation student of Senior Grandmaster Edmund K. Parker, the father of American Kenpo Karate, and attained the rank of Black Belt in 1968.

David lived in Napa, California for over five years before recently relocating to Tucson, Arizona.

His current interests include his relationship with his mate, Susan, gardening projects at his home in the desert, the study of psychology as it relates to esteem, and superficial explorations into history.

He abhors war and its aftermath.

David wishes all of us a peaceful, rewarding, happy, fulfilling experience while we are alive, and endeavors to make the lives of others better than they may now be.

Bonus Material: three additional chapters about David's early life from childhood through boot camp can be found on our website at this unlisted address http://www.LovingHealing.com/dwpextra

COMBAT HISTORY—EXPEDITIONS—AWARDS RECORD

COMBAT HISTORY—EXPEDITIONS

DATE OF ENTRY	DETAILS	DATES FROM (ON)—	DATES TO—	SIGNATURE
23Oct66	Participated in operations against Communist Insurgent (Viet Cong) Guerrilla Forces in the Republic of Vietnam	23Oct66		
1Dec66	Participated in Operation Rio Blanco Quang Ngai RVN Shark	20Nov66	27Nov66	W. M. Gibbs ByDir
16Feb67	Participated in Operation Trinity, RVN	30Jan67	1Feb67	J. E. Perkins ByDir
16Apr67	Participated in Operation Boone, RVN	1Apr67	7Apr67	J. E. Perkins ByDir
17May67	Participated in Operation Union, Quang Nam, RVN	21Apr67	5May67	J. E. Perkins ByDir
5Jun67	Participated in Operation Duvall, Quang Nam, RVN	19May67	24May67	J. E. Perkins ByDir
5Jun67	Participated in Operation Union II, Quang Tin, RVN	2Jun67	4Jun67	J. E. Perkins ByDir
6Jun67	WIA NE, GSW, left hand	20Dec66		J. E. Perkins ByDir
2Jul67	Participated in Operation Arizona, Quang Nam, RVN	18Jun67	23Jun67	J. E. Perkins ByDir
8Jul67	Op Elliot, Quang Nam, RVN	5Jul67	6Jul67	J. E. Perkins By dir
11Jul67	Op Sween, Quang Nam, RVN	6Jul67	9Jul67	J. E. Perkins By dir
31Jul67	Op Geb, Quang Nam, RVN	13Jul67	18Jul67	
31Jul67	Op Boulder-Pecos, Quang Nam, RVN	19Jul67	27Jul67	
31Jul67	Op Stockton, Quang Nam, RVN	27Jul67	29Jul67	J. J. Karras ByDir

AWARDS

DESCRIPTION	STARS, DEVICES	DATE APPROVED	APPROVED BY	DATE MEDAL ISSUED	SIGNATURE
NAT DEF		5 MAY 1966	SECNAV NOTE 1650 OF 5 MAY 1966		N. O. Cofield CO
VSM	w/*	23Oct66	SECNAVNOTE 1650 of 14Oct65		W. M. Gibbs ByDir
VCM		23Apr67	CO 1/7, 1stMarDiv		J. E. Perkins ByDir
PH		20Dec66	CG, 1stMarDiv	19Jun67	J. E. Perkins ByDir

EMBOSSED PLATE IMPRESSION

POWELL, DAVID W.   M 2269994
NAME (Last)   (First)   (Middle)   SERVICE NO.

NAVMC 118(9)-PD (REV. 1-63) SUPERSEDES 11-55 EDITION WHICH WILL BE USED.   U.S. GOVERNMENT PRINTING OFFICE : 1963 OF—672066

Combat history – Expeditions – Awards Record

THIS IS AN IMPORTANT RECORD
SAFEGUARD IT.

1. LAST NAME - FIRST NAME - MIDDLE NAME	2. SERVICE NUMBER	3. SOCIAL SECURITY NUMBER
POWELL, David Warren	2269994	561 52 7514

4. DEPARTMENT, COMPONENT AND BRANCH OR CLASS	5a. GRADE, RATE OR RANK	b. PAY GRADE	6. DATE OF RANK	DAY	MONTH	YEAR
USMC	CPL	E-4		01	06	67

7. U. S. CITIZEN	8. PLACE OF BIRTH (City and State or Country)	9. DATE OF BIRTH	DAY	MONTH	YEAR
☒ YES ☐ NO	Los Angeles, Calif		18	08	41

10a. SELECTIVE SERVICE NUMBER	b. SELECTIVE SERVICE LOCAL BOARD NUMBER, CITY, COUNTY, STATE AND ZIP CODE	c. DATE INDUCTED	DAY	MONTH	YEAR
4 91 41 346	Bd#91 Pasadena, Los Angeles, Calif 91107	Not Applicable			

11. TYPE OF TRANSFER OR DISCHARGE	8. STATION OR INSTALLATION AT WHICH EFFECTED
Transferred to Marine Corps Reserve	MCB CamPen Calif

c. REASON AND AUTHORITY	d. EFFECTIVE DATE	DAY	MONTH	YEAR
202- Expiration of Enlistment par 13258 Marine Corps Parsonnel Manual		11	04	68

12. LAST DUTY ASSIGNMENT AND MAJOR COMMAND	13a. CHARACTER OF SERVICE	b. TYPE OF CERTIFICATE ISSUED
28thMar 5thMarDiv FMF CamPen Calif CoL 3rdBn	HONORABLE	None

14. DISTRICT, AREA COMMAND OR CORPS TO WHICH RESERVIST TRANSFERRED	15. REENLISTMENT CODE
Marine Corps Automated Services Center Kansas City, Missouri	RE-1

16. TERMINAL DATE OF RESERVE / UNFB'S OBLIGATION			17. CURRENT ACTIVE SERVICE OTHER THAN BY INDUCTION a. SOURCE OF ENTRY	b. TERM OF SERVICE (Years)	c. DATE OF ENTRY		
DAY	MONTH	YEAR			DAY	MONTH	YEAR
08	03	72	☒ ENLISTED (First Enlistment) ☐ ENLISTED (Prior Service) ☐ OTHER ☐ REENLISTED	02	12	04	66

18. PRIOR REGULAR ENLISTMENTS	19. GRADE, RATE OR RANK AT TIME OF ENTRY INTO CURRENT ACTIVE SVC	20. PLACE OF ENTRY INTO CURRENT ACTIVE SERVICE (City and State)
None	P/T (E-1)	Los Angeles, Calif

21. HOME OF RECORD AT TIME OF ENTRY INTO ACTIVE SERVICE (Street, RFD, City, County, State and ZIP Code)	22.	STATEMENT OF SERVICE	YEARS	MONTHS	DAYS
155 S. Daisy Ave. Pasadena, Los Angeles, Calif 91107		(1) NET SERVICE THIS PERIOD	02	02	00
	CREDITABLE FOR BASIC PAY PURPOSES	(2) OTHER SERVICE	00	02	03
		(3) TOTAL (Line (1) plus Line (2))	02	02	03
23a. SPECIALTY NUMBER & TITLE	b. RELATED CIVILIAN OCCUPATION AND D.O.T. NUMBER	b. TOTAL ACTIVE SERVICE	02	00	00
0351 AntiTnkAsltMan	0-56.54 Proof Director Small Arms (Firearms)	c. FOREIGN AND/OR SEA SERVICE	01	00	26

24. DECORATIONS, MEDALS, BADGES, COMMENDATIONS, CITATIONS AND CAMPAIGN RIBBONS AWARDED OR AUTHORIZED
National Defense Service Medal; Vietnamese Service Medal with 1 Star; Vietnamese Campaign Medal with Device (1960-); Purple Heart Medal; Expert Badge, Rifle

25. EDUCATION AND TRAINING COMPLETED
High School 4- Vocational College 1- Business Administration

26a. NON-PAY PERIODS/TIME LOST (Preceding Two Years)	b. DAYS ACCRUED LEAVE PAID	27a. INSURANCE IN FORCE (NSLI or USGLI)	b. AMOUNT OF ALLOTMENT	c. MONTH ALLOTMENT DISCONTINUED
None	Twenty-five (25) days	☐ YES ☒ NO	$ N/A	N/A
	28. VA CLAIM NUMBER	29. SERVICEMAN'S GROUP LIFE INSURANCE COVERAGE		
	c. N/A	☒ $10,000 ☐ $5,000 ☐ NONE		

30. REMARKS
Enlisted in the United States Marine Corps Is undecided about reenlistment Good Conduct Medal Period Commences 12 April 1966

31. PERMANENT ADDRESS FOR MAILING PURPOSES AFTER TRANSFER OR DISCHARGE (Street, RFD, City, County, State and ZIP Code)	32. SIGNATURE OF PERSON BEING TRANSFERRED OR DISCHARGED
See Item #21	*David W. Powell*
33. TYPED NAME, GRADE AND TITLE OF AUTHORIZING OFFICER	34. SIGNATURE OF OFFICER AUTHORIZED TO SIGN
R. C. MOORE 1stLt ExecO	*R.D. Moore*

DD FORM 214 MC (1968) PREVIOUS EDITIONS OF THIS FORM ARE OBSOLETE. ARMED FORCES OF THE UNITED STATES REPORT OF TRANSFER OR DISCHARGE S/N-0101-880-4301   INDIV-1

DD214 (Discharge Papers)

Study Guide

The purpose of this Study Guide is to highlight the symptoms and consequences of PTSD in general using David Powell as a specific case. It is my hope that this approach will be of benefit to therapists and counselors-in-training, ministers, lay advocates of veterans, and those who interact frequently with victims of traumatic stress. In the course of reading the story it is easy to get caught up in the action. The Study Guide is designed to help wring out as much of the etiology of PTSD from David's narrative as possible. I would like to acknowledge Rene Ely, LMFT for providing the impetus to develop this Study Guide.   —Victor R. Volkman, Editor

Foreword

1. The Department of Defense reported neuropsychiatric causualty rate for Vietnam was actually lower than previous conflicts. List and explain some reasons.

2. List at least three symptoms and three negative personal outcomes common to PTSD sufferers.

3. What were the impacts on soldiers of fixed length tours of duty DEROS ("Date of Expected Return from Over Seas Duty")?

4. What are some advantages of a slower return to the civilian world direct from the battlefield?

Chapter 1

1. List feelings, emotions, sensations, attitudes or pains (FESAPs) associated with David's incident of "freezing under fire".

2. David experiences subjective time slowing down during some incidents. Has this phenomenon of "bullet time" ever happened to you? (for example, during a motor vehicle accident or other physical crisis).

3. What incident is at the root of David's fear of open spaces?

4. How does David's startle reaction serve to protect him on the battlefield?

Chapter 2

1. How does David justify his killings of the enemy?

2. What new promise does he make about any future killing?

3. What phobia develops from the helicopter landing zone incident? Discuss the proportion or frequency of phobias you think might have primary incidents like this.

4. What intentions and counter-intentions were inside this incident?

Chapter 3

1. How does David react to his third killing in light of his earlier promise?
2. What decision does David make during the stressful confrontation with Private Allen?
3. What FESAPs surround this incident?
4. How can a decision tied to an unfulfilled intention stick with you for years? Think of an example in your life or in popular fiction.

Chapter 4

1. In *The Power of Ritual* (2000), Rachel Pollack says that a ritual "Connects us to each other, to nature, to the cycles and rhythms of life," she explains. "It opens our heart to love and to intense emotion-sadness and longing as well as joy. And it opens a space for what we call the sacred or spirituality to enter our lives." List examples of ritual that you have witnessed or used yourself. What is it about ritual that generates the feeling of safety?

2. In *Life Skills* (2005), Marian Volkman describes the quality level of a relationship being defined by the balance of the elements of Communication, Comprehension, and Affection (after Gerbode, 1995). What element was missing from the letters between David and his wife that would produce a decline in the relationship?

Chapter 5

1. What other unwanted characteristic develops out of David's attempt to control his unpredictable rage?

2. What incidents cause David to become obsessed with cleaning and maintaining his weaponry?

3. In *Beyond Trauma, 2nd Edition* (2005), Gerbode defines the *flows* of a traumatic incident:

> "A person can have charge not only on what has been done to him, but also on what he has done to others, what others have done to others, and what he has done to himself. When a viewer [client, seeking to resolve traumatic stress thru TIR or related techniques] has a charged incident that contains one of these flows, it is quite likely he will also have similar incidents on other flows that are also charged." (p. 11)

List the flows involved in the incidents surrounding this chapter: David witnesses the death of "Bear", David attacks the blindfolded sniper, David witnesses men fragging themselves, he witnesses civilians killed in unprovoked assaults.

Chapter 6

1. What effects of PTSD are present in David's encounter with Kathy in the Honolulu airport?

2. What is missing from David's interaction with Kathy in the realms of Communication, Comprehension, and Affection? What do you think the chances are of maintain a healthy relationship with missing components?

3. Which incidents so far in the book have contributed to David's mistrust of any type of authority figure?

Chapter 7

1. What are the emotional and physical risks of befriending a colleague in a dangerous situation? How well does isolation work as a coping mechanism?

2. What decisions does David make which are tied to the death of his friend Kenny?

3. What secondary emotions are added each time a startle-response is triggered?

   4. Which incidents in this chapter contribute to David's growing mistrust for authority?

Chapter 8

   1. What unfulfilled intention(s) does David have upon returning to the USA to finish out his enlistment?

   2. What counter-intentions does he create against the background of unfulfilled intentions?

Chapter 9

   1. What prior incident and embedded decision prevents David from confronting his supervisor about keeping his job?

   2. What PTSD symptoms are emerging in this chapter? List specific examples.

   3. What specific incidents led to David's fear of abandonment and how does it impact his relationships?

Chapter 10

   1. What new PTSD symptoms are emerging and how does David attempt to suppress them?

   2. What incidents and decisions resulting from them make it extremely difficult for David to confront his boss about overdue commissions or loans?

   3. How do recurring PTSD symptoms create their own 'new' incidents? List at least two examples from this chapter.

Chapter 11

   1. What PTSD symptoms begin to abate after David enters therapy?

   2. TIR is an *exposure-based* technique. What other exposure-based techniques are currently in use?

   3. Read the TIR FAQ http://www.tir.org/metapsy/tirfaq.htm and compare TIR with another technique you have studied.

Chapter 12

1. What private victories has David had since completing TIR?

2. Read Gerbode's "Critical Issues in Trauma Resolution" at
   http://www.tir.org/metapsy/issues.htm
   A. According to Gerbode's theory, anamnesis (recovery of repressed memories) is required for permanent resolution of
   trauma. How well does David's recovery fit this model?
   B. See if you can re-construct a simplified Traumatic Incident
   Network based on David's incidents (or some other case you
   have studied previously).

3. List some external restimulators of David's theme of "difficulty
   in confronting people" that he grappled with.

Suggested Reading

"About Post-Traumatic Stress Disorder" (2003). South Deerfield, MA: Channing-Bete Co. www.channing-bete.com (16pp booklet).

Gerbode, F.A. (1989). *Beyond Psychology: an Introduction to Metapsychology*, 3rd Ed. (1995) Menlo Park, CA: IRM Press.

Gerbode, F.A. (2005). "Traumatic Incident Reduction" in Garrick and Williams [ed.] *Trauma Treatment Techniques: Innovative trends.* New York, NY: Haworth Press.

Mason, P. (1990). *Recovering form the War: A Woman's Guide to Helping your Vietnam Vet, Your Family and Yourself.* New York, NY: Viking Adult.

Meichenbaum, D. (2003) *A Clinical Handbook/Practical Therapist Manual for Assessing and Treating Adults with Post-Traumatic Stress Disorder (PTSD).* The Melissa Institute.

Valentine, P. and Smith, Thomas E. "Evaluating Traumatic Incident Reduction Therapy with Female Inmates: a Randomized Controlled Clinical Trial." *Research on Social Work Practice*, v. 11, no. 1, pp. 40-52, January 2001, ISSN: 1049-7315.

Valentine, P. "Traumatic Incident Reduction I: Traumatized Women Inmates: Particulars of Practice and Research", *Journal of Offender Rehabilitation* Vol. 31(3-4): 1-15, 2000.

Van Der Kolk, B. et al. (1999) *Traumatic Stress: Effects of Overwhelming Experience on Mind, Body and Society.* Guilford Press.

Volkman, Marian (2005) *Life Skills: Improve the Quality of Your Life with Metapsychology.* Ann Arbor, MI. Loving Healing Press.

Volkman, Victor (2005) *Beyond Trauma: Conversations on Traumatic Incident Reduction, 2nd Ed.* Ann Arbor, MI. Loving Healing Press.

Volkman, Victor (2005) *Traumatic Incident Reduction: Research and Results.* Ann Arbor, MI. Loving Healing Press.

FAQ from the
National Center for PTSD

What is PTSD?

Post-Traumatic Stress Disorder, or PTSD, is a psychiatric disorder that can occur following the experience or witnessing of life-threatening events such as military combat, natural disasters, terrorist incidents, serious accidents, abuse (sexual, physical, emotional, ritual), and violent personal assaults like rape. People who suffer from PTSD often relive the experience through nightmares and flashbacks, have difficulty sleeping, and feel detached or estranged, and these symptoms can be severe enough and last long enough to significantly impair the person's daily life.

PTSD is marked by clear biological changes as well as psychological symptoms. PTSD is complicated by the fact that it frequently occurs in conjunction with related disorders such as depression, substance abuse, problems of memory and cognition, and other problems of physical and mental health. The disorder is also associated with impairment of the person's ability to function in social or family life, including occupational instability, marital problems and divorces, family discord, and difficulties in parenting.

Understanding PTSD

PTSD is not a new disorder. There are written accounts of similar symptoms that go back to ancient times, and there is clear documentation in the historical medical literature starting with the Civil War, when a PTSD-like disorder was known as "Da Costa's Syndrome." There are particularly good descriptions of posttraumatic stress symptoms in the medical literature on combat veterans of World War II and on Holocaust survivors.

Careful research and documentation of PTSD began in earnest after the Vietnam War. The National Vietnam Veterans Readjustment Study estimated in 1988 that the prevalence of PTSD in that group was 15.2% at that time and that 30% had experienced the disorder at some point since returning from Vietnam.

PTSD has subsequently been observed in all veteran populations that have been studied, including World War II, Korean conflict, and Persian Gulf populations, and in United Nations peacekeeping forces deployed to other war zones around the world. There are remarkably similar findings of PTSD in military veterans in other countries. For example, Australian Vietnam veterans experience many of the same symptoms that American Vietnam veterans experience.

PTSD is not only a problem for veterans, however. Although there are unique cultural- and gender-based aspects of the disorder, it occurs in men and women, adults and children, Western and non-Western cultural groups, and all socioeconomic strata. A national study of American civilians conducted in 1995 estimated that the lifetime prevalence of PTSD was 5% in men and 10% in women. A revision of this study done in 2005, reports that PTSD occurs in about 8% of all Americans.

How does PTSD develop?

Most people who are exposed to a traumatic, stressful event experience some of the symptoms of PTSD in the days and weeks following exposure. Available data suggest that about 8% of men and 20% of women go on to develop PTSD, and roughly 30% of these individuals develop a chronic form that persists throughout their lifetimes.

The course of chronic PTSD usually involves periods of symptom increase followed by remission or decrease, although some individuals may experience symptoms that are unremitting and severe. Some older veterans, who report a lifetime of only mild symptoms, experience significant increases in symptoms following retirement, severe medical illness in themselves or their spouses, or reminders of their military service (such as reunions or media broadcasts of the anniversaries of war events).

How is PTSD assessed?

In recent years, a great deal of research has been aimed at developing and testing reliable assessment tools. It is generally thought that the best way to diagnose PTSD-or any psychiatric disorder, for that matter-is to combine findings from structured interviews and questionnaires with physiological assessments. A multi-method approach especially helps address concerns that some patients might be either denying or exaggerating their symptoms.

How common is PTSD?

An estimated 7.8 percent of Americans will experience PTSD at some point in their lives, with women (10.4%) twice as likely as men (5%) to develop PTSD. About 3.6 percent of U.S. adults aged 18 to 54 (5.2 million people) have PTSD during the course of a given year. This represents a small portion of those who have experienced at least one traumatic event; 60.7% of men and 51.2% of women reported at least one traumatic event. The traumatic events most often associated with PTSD for men are rape, combat exposure, childhood neglect, and childhood physical abuse. The most traumatic events for women are rape, sexual molestation, physical attack, being threatened with a weapon, and childhood physical abuse.

About 30 percent of the men and women who have spent time in war zones experience PTSD. An additional 20 to 25 percent have had partial PTSD at some point in their lives. More than half of all male Vietnam veterans and almost half of all female Vietnam veterans have experienced "clinically serious stress reaction symptoms." PTSD has also been detected among veterans of the Gulf War, with some estimates running as high as 8 percent.

Who is most likely to develop PTSD?

1.   Those who experience greater stressor magnitude and intensity, unpredictability, uncontrollability, sexual (as opposed to nonsexual) victimization, real or perceived responsibility, and betrayal

2.   Those with prior vulnerability factors such as genetics, early age of onset and longer-lasting childhood trauma, lack of functional social support, and concurrent stressful life events

3.   Those who report greater perceived threat or danger, suffering, upset, terror, and horror or fear

4.   Those with a social environment that produces shame, guilt, stigmatization, or self-hatred

What are the consequences associated with PTSD?

PTSD is associated with a number of distinctive neurobiological and physiological changes. PTSD may be associated with stable neurobiological alterations in both the central and autonomic nervous systems, such as altered brainwave activity, decreased volume of the hippocampus, and abnormal activation of the amygdala. Both the hippocampus and the amygdala are involved in the processing and integration of memory. The amygdala has also been found to be involved in coordinating the body's fear response.

Psychophysiological alterations associated with PTSD include hyperarousal of the sympathetic nervous system, increased sensitivity of the startle reflex, and sleep abnormalities.

People with PTSD tend to have abnormal levels of key hormones involved in the body's response to stress. Thyroid function also seems to be enhanced in people with PTSD. Some studies have shown that cortisol levels in those with PTSD are lower than normal and epinephrine and norepinephrine levels are higher than normal. People with PTSD also continue to produce higher than normal levels of natural opiates after the trauma has passed. An important finding is that the neurohormonal changes seen in PTSD are distinct from, and actually opposite to, those seen in major depression. The distinctive profile associated with PTSD is also seen in individuals who have both PTSD and depression.

PTSD is associated with the increased likelihood of co-occurring psychiatric disorders. In a large-scale study, 88 percent of men and 79 percent of women with PTSD met criteria for another psychiatric disorder. The co-occurring disorders most prevalent for men with PTSD were alcohol abuse or dependence (51.9 percent), major depressive episodes (47.9 percent), conduct disorders (43.3 percent), and drug abuse and dependence (34.5 percent). The disorders most frequently comorbid with PTSD among women were major depressive disorders (48.5 percent), simple phobias (29 percent), social phobias (28.4 percent), and alcohol abuse/dependence (27.9 percent).

PTSD also significantly impacts psychosocial functioning, independent of comorbid conditions. For instance, Vietnam veterans with PTSD were found to have profound and pervasive problems in their daily lives. These included problems in family and other interpersonal relationships, problems with employment, and involvement with the criminal justice system.

Headaches, gastrointestinal complaints, immune system problems, dizziness, chest pain, and discomfort in other parts of the body are common in people with PTSD. Often, medical doctors treat the symptoms without being aware that they stem from PTSD.

What treatments are available for PTSD?

Elements common to many treatment modalities for PTSD include education, exposure, exploration of feelings and beliefs, and coping skills training. Additionally, the most common treatment modalities include cognitive-behavioral treatment, pharmacotherapy, EMDR, group treatment, and psychodynamic treatment.

For a further discussion, please go to
http://www.ncptsd.va.gov/facts/treatment/fs_treatment.html

I am an American Veteran. Who do I contact for help with PTSD?

You can contact your local VA Hospital or Veterans Center or call the VA Health Benefits Service Center toll free at 1-877-222-VETS!

For online help, please see
http://www.ncptsd.va.gov/facts/veterans/fs_treatment_programs.html.

As an American Veteran, how do I file a claim for disability due to PTSD?

A determination of "service-connected" disability for PTSD is made by the Compensation and Pension Service—an arm of VA's Veterans Benefits Administration. The clinicians who provide care for veterans in VA's specialized PTSD clinics and Vet Centers do not make this decision. A formal request ("claim") must be filed by the veteran using forms provided by the VA's Veterans Benefits Administration. After the forms are completely submitted, the veteran must complete interviews concerning her or his "social history" (a review of family, work, and educational experiences before, during, and after military service) and "psychiatric status" (a review of past and current psychological symptoms, and of traumatic experiences during military service). The forms and information about the application process can be obtained by Benefits Officers at any VA Medical Center, Outpatient Clinic, or Regional Office.

The process of applying for a VA disability for PTSD can take several months, and can be both complicated and quite stressful. The Veteran's Service Organizations provide "Service Officers" at no cost to help veterans and family members pursue VA disability claims. Service Officers are familiar with every step in the application and interview process, and can provide both technical guidance and moral support. In addition, some

Service Officers particularly specialize in assisting veterans with PTSD disability claims. Even if a veteran has not been a member of a specific Veterans Service Organization, the veteran still can request the assistance of a Service Officer working for that organization. In order to get representation by a qualified and helpful Service Officer, you can directly contact the local office of any Veterans Service Organization -- or ask for recommendations from other veterans who have applied for VA disability, or from a PTSD specialist at a VA PTSD clinic or a Vet Center.

For online information,
http://www.ncptsd.va.gov/facts/veterans/fs_help_for_vets.html

For more information call the PTSD Information Line at (802) 296-6300 or send email to ncptsd@ncptsd.org..

Appendix C

Vietnam/Military Glossary

Glossary items from Wikipedia (http://en.wikipedia.org/) unless otherwise noted

A-Gunner (Assistant Gunner): many fire teams including rockets, mortar, machine gun are designated as Gunner and Assistant Gunner. The A-Gunner's role exists completely to support the mission of the Gunner by carrying spare parts, ammunition, assisting reloading and targeting and so on.

ARVN (Army of the Republic of Vietnam): a military component of the armed forces of the Republic of Vietnam (commonly known as South Vietnam). At the end of the Vietnam War, after the fall of Saigon, it was dissolved, and hundreds of thousands of its members were sent to reeducation camps by the communist government.

DMZ (Demilitarized Zone): In military terms, a demilitarized zone (DMZ) is an area, usually the frontier or boundary between two or more groups, where military activity is not permitted, usually by treaty or other agreement. Often the demilitarized zone lies upon a line of control and forms a de-facto international border.

Fragging: "Frag incidents" or "fragging" was soldier slang in Vietnam for the killing of strict, unpopular and aggressive officers and NCO's [Non-Commissioned Officers]. The word apparently originated from enlisted men using fragmentation grenades to kill commanders. We use the word here to include causing intentional harm to a fellow soldier of your own unit—yourself or others. Congressional hearings on fraggings held in 1973 estimated that roughly 3% of officer and non-com deaths in Vietnam between 1961 and 1972 were a result of fraggings. But these figures were only for killings committed with grenades, and didn't include officer deaths from automatic weapons fire, handguns and knifings. The Army's Judge Advocate General's Corps estimated that only 10% of fragging attempts resulted in anyone going to trial. (source: Kevin Keating)

Grunt: The US Marines divide themselves into two camps. Those who do the fighting are "grunts." Those who do not are POGs, "persons other than grunts". POGs are the support element of the Marine Corps. To a grunt, a POG is anyone with access to a hot meal and a shower and at night beds down in a cot. They resupply the grunts with food, fuel and water. They make repairs. They perform the thousands of jobs that make fighting possible. It is the grunts, however, who do the fighting, the killing and, most often, the dying. They consider themselves modern-day warriors. (Source: John Murphy)

Gunny (Gunnery Sergeant): in rank above Staff Sergeant and below Master Sergeant. This nickname is usually regarded as a title of esteem, and is generally acceptable for use in all situations except formal and ceremonial ones. Use of the term by lower-ranking personnel, however, remains at the Gunnery Sergeant's discretion.

Medevac (Medical Evacuation): A MEDEVAC is a military acronym for "medical evacuation." A MEDEVAC is also a helicopter used as an ambulance. This permits the rapid transport of seriously injured persons, particularly trauma patients, from the scene of the accident to the hospital. The US military pioneered this lifesaving technique during the Korean War. Many patients transported by MEDEVAC are taken to a specialized hospital known as a trauma center.

New Guy (F—ing New Guy): In Vietnam, what you didn't know could get you killed or mutilated in a hurry. The FNG could draw enemy fire, trip booby traps, or fail to help anyone near him due to his lack of combat experience.

NCO (Non-Com, Non-Commissioned Officer): literally a non-commissioned member of an armed force who has been given authority by a commissioned officer. The non-commissioned officer corps is the junior management of the military. Typically NCOs serve as administrative personnel, as advisors to the officer corps, and as both supervisors of, and advocates for, the lower-ranking enlisted personnel. In the Marine Corps, all ranks of Sergeant are termed NCOs, as are Corporals in the Army and Marines.

NVA (North Vietnamese Army): The People's Army of Vietnam was the regularly trained and organized military force of the North Vietnamese government during the Vietnam War. The PAVN typically operated in regimental strength but sometimes formed elements as small as companies. Unlike the Viet Cong, the PAVN was not a guerilla force.

Point (Walking Point): A reconnaissance or patrol unit that moves ahead of an advance party or guard, or that follows a rear guard. The position occupied by such a unit or guard: "A team of Rangers were walking point at the outset of the operation." Point is one of the most dangerous positions of combat.

Short-timer: Contrary to what it sounds like, a short-timer is a combat veteran very near the end of his tour of duty. Men in such a position would rarely take any avoidable risks. Contrast with the FNG [F—ing New Guy], a new arrival who is dangerous to everyone until he learns the ropes.

TAOR (Tactical Area of Operational Responsibility): In conversation, it would be abbreviated to just "AO" (ay-oh).

Victor Charlie (VC): military phonetic alphabetic representation of "VC", used as a radio codeword. VC is an abbreviation for Viet Cong (see below).

Viet Cong: The National Front for the Liberation of Vietnam or National Liberation Front was known to American soldiers in Vietnam as the Viet Cong—from a contraction for the Vietnamese phrase Viet Nam Cong San, or "Vietnamese Communist."

This originally derogatory phrase was used by the Republic of Vietnam (RVN) government of South Vietnam under President Ngo Dinh Diem to describe his political opponents, many of whom were Communists, starting after the partition of Vietnam between the RVN in the South and the Democratic Republic of Vietnam (DRV) in the North which took place in 1954. Later, during the Vietnam War, the RVN and the United States government used this expression to refer to the National Front for the Liberation of Vietnam (NLF) and its guerrilla army, the People's Liberation Armed Forces (PLAF). (The NLF and the PLAF themselves never used this expression to refer to themselves, and always asserted that they were a national front of all anti-RVN forces, communist or not.) It is this use of "Viet Cong" that most people in the United States and Europe are most familiar.

Index

Coping with Physical Loss and Disability:
A Workbook by Rick Ritter, MSW

Do You Have A Loved One with Disabilities?

This workbook provides more than 50 questions and exercises designed to empower those with physical loss and disability to better understand and accept their ongoing processes of loss and recovery. The exercises in *Coping with Physical Loss and Disability* were distilled from ten years of clinical social work experience with clients suffering from quadriplegia, paraplegia, amputation(s), cancer, severe burns, AIDs, hepatitis, lupus, and neuromuscular disorders arising from. Whether the physical loss arises from accidents, injury, surgery, or disease, the techniques in this new workbook are guaranteed to improve functioning and well-being.

Praise *for Coping with Physical Loss and Disability*

"This workbook is a very good stimulus for focusing on issues that are crucial for better coping with loss and disability."
—Beni R. Jakob, PhD, Israeli Arthritis Foundation (INBAR)

"This workbook is a tremendous resource that is practical and easy to use. The author shows his connection with this material in a way from which we can all benefit." —Geneva Reynaga-Abiko, PsyD,
Clinical Psychologist, Urbana-Champaign Counseling Center

"To date I have not seen another tool that can help people who have disabilities become self-aware and adjust to their new lives as well as this workbook does. This workbook can help them to see how they still have strengths ad abilities and move beyond being disabled to reestablish their self-acceptance and functionality." —Ian Landry, MSW, RSW

"Rick Ritter is able to provide us with an insightful road map to the growth process of individuals experiencing physical loss. As clinicians we often need to provide support to those who have experienced much more loss than we ever can imagine. This workbook is a masterpiece in helping us accomplish that proficiency." —Darlene DiGorio-Hevner, LCSW

Loving Healing Press

Loving Healing Press
5145 Pontiac Trail
Ann Arbor, MI 48105

(734)662-6864

info@LovingHealing.com

124 pp — $17.95 Retail
ISBN-13 978-1-932690-18-7
Includes bibliog., resources, and index.

http:/www.PhysicalLoss.com

Beyond Trauma:
Conversations on Traumatic Incident Reduction, 2ⁿᵈ Ed.

Exclusive offer for readers of *My Tour in Hell*

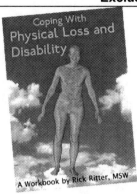  

Share the power of Loving Healing Press Books

Order direct from the publisher with this form and save!

Order Form – 15% Discount Off List Price!

Ship To:

_____
Name

_____
Address

_____
Address

_____   _____
City   State

_____
District   Country   Zip/Post code

_____
Daytime phone #

_____
email address

☐ **VISA**   ☐ **MasterCard**   ☐ check payable to
Loving Healing Press

_____   _____/_____
Card #   Expires

_____
Signature

Beyond Trauma, 2nd Ed _____ x $19.50 = _____

Coping w/Phys. Loss _____ x $15 = _____

My Tour in Hell _____ x $23 = _____
(Hardcover Ed.)

Subtotal = _____

Residents of Michigan: 6% tax = _____

Shipping charge (see below) _____

Your Total _$_____

Shipping price _per copy_ via:

☐ Priority Mail (+ $3.50)   ☐ Int'l Airmail (+ $4)   ☐ USA MediaMail/4th Class (+ $2)

Fax Order Form back to (734)663-6861 or
Mail to LHP, 5145 Pontiac Trail, Ann Arbor, MI 48105

Printed in the United States
53027LVS00001BA/189